ARCHITECTURE IS ELEMENTARY.

Visual Thinking Through Architectural Concepts

Dan

Day 7, 1993

Use your eyes to see more than the surface.

Utah Heritage Foundation

Through an innovative school program for fourth graders which gives credence to the idea that architecture has a valid place in the curriculum for all students, Utah Heritage Foundation provided the inspiration for this book. Generous contributions to the Utah Heritage Foundation made possible the research for and writing of the first manuscript.

Utah Heritage Foundation and Adele W. Weiler received, in May 1985, a Preservation Honor Award from the National Trust for Historic Preservation "for the excellent and innovative school programs created under the direction of Adele W. Weiler and sponsored by the Utah Heritage Foundation, which take preservation into the classrooms and the neighborhoods and reach 5,000 students each year."

Major contributors:

Edna Wattis Dumke

Utah State Office of Education

Also contributing:

R. Harold Burton

Greater Cincinnati Fund

Blanche B. Rich Foundation

ARCHITECTURE IS ELEMENTARY

Visual Thinking Through Architectural Concepts

NATHAN B. WINTERS,
AUTHOR AND ILLUSTRATOR

GIBBS SMITH, PUBLISHER
Peregrine Smith Books
Salt Lake City

Design by Ray Morales

Manufactured in the
United States of America.

93   7

Library of Congress Cataloging
in Publication Data

Winters, Nathan B., 1937-
Architecture is elementary.

1. Architecture.   2. Visual perception.   I. Title.
NA2500.W56   1985   720'.1   84-23523
ISBN 0-87906-186-8

TABLE OF CONTENTS

Level Five

Level Six

Level Seven

ACKNOWLEDGEMENTS

Those who have influenced the contents of this text are gratefully acknowledged:

Charles B. Stubbs, Art Specialist, Utah State Office of Education;

Ivan E. Cornia, Supervisor of Art, Davis County Schools;

Darrel B. Allington, Art Specialist, Granite School District;

Calvin W. Taylor, Professor, University of Utah;

Patrick J. Eddington, Art Instructor, Salt Lake City School District;

Barbara Beus, Art Instructor, Berlin, Germany;

Robert Olpin, Chairman, Department of Art, University of Utah;

Heidi Casey, consultant, educator and colleague;

Gibbs M. Smith, publisher and consultant;

Madge Baird, editor, proved this book's educational power in her own life and perceptions;

Raye Graham first realized the need;

Students of art and architecture, University of Utah.

Illustration and layout assistance:

Ray Morales;

Jana Winters.

J. Scott Knudsen

Typing of manuscript:

Susan, Jana, and Emily Winters.

Illustrations were reprinted by permission from the following:

Architecture: Form, Space and Order by Francis D. K. Ching. Published by Van Nostrand Reinhold: p. 148, figs. 28.5 and 28.6; p. 216, fig 45.6.

Arts and Ideas by William Fleming. Copyright © 1980 by Holt, Rinehardt, and Winston. Reprinted with permission of CBS College Publishing: p. 77, fig 22b.10; p. 80, fig. 22b.19; p. 114, fig. 23.8.

Quayle House packet published by Utah Heritage Foundation: pp. 9-11.

''Experiments in the Visual Perception of Texture'' by Bela Julesz. *Scientific American*, April 1975. Reprinted by permission of W.H. Freeman and Company Publishers: p. 188, figs. 38.3-38.7.

Urban Space: A Brief History of the City Square by French. Copyright © 1978 by Kendall/Hunt Publishing Company. Reprinted by permission of Kendall/Hunt Publishing Company: p. 212, figs. 44.2, 44.4; p. 213, fig. 44.6.

"Ruskin said: 'Great nations write their autobiographies in three manuscripts, the book of their deeds, the book of their words and the book of their art. Not one of these books can be understood unless we read the two others, but of the three the only trustworthy one is the last.' On the whole I think this is true. If I had to say which was telling the truth about society, a speech by a minister of housing or the actual buildings put up in his time, I should believe the buildings.'—Kenneth Clark

Why Study Architecture? Years of research indicate that the lay public has not grown much beyond the fourth grade level in visual literacy. The danger in leaving our culture dangling at the fourth grade level visually, is that it is a human tendency not to miss that which we do not know. Quality, then, when not imagined or recognized, is not even missed—much to the joy of mediocrity and her friends congregating on each corner.

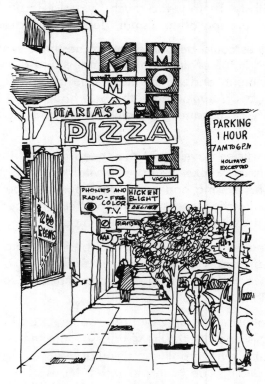

1.1.

One of the basic maturities of education is "environmental." The root words of *environment* declare it to mean the sum total of influences which modify and determine the development of life or character. In all of the earth's history, no culture—no time—has been more in need, been more concerned with environment. We want to preserve rare species, to have clean air and pure water, to enjoy rich forests and wilderness areas. The *built* environment is one of the major environmental concerns of the twentieth and twenty-first centuries. The built environment comes under attack from two flanks—historical and aesthetic. The historical attack is actually *anti*-historical. Many of our finest buildings have become rare species, in need of protection. Natural predators in the form of business, government, building codes, demolition crews and remodelers, and modernizers worship at the altar of "progress," as they faithfully destroy our cultural heritage.

Toward the end of chapter eight in *The Grapes of Wrath,* John Steinbeck's midwest farmers who were trapped in the dust bowls of devastating drought during the already difficult years of the Great Depression, were being forced to leave for California. As they loaded their small pickup truck with the things they needed to take with them, they were forced to leave many precious items behind, such as the old family books tracing back four generations, paintings and dishes, and collectibles. As they looked at what must be left behind, one of the older ladies pondered, "How can we live without our lives? How will we know it's us without our past?" This is one of the questions we must ask, too, as we become more and more aware of our inalienable rights to a heritage.

Along with this right to have a rich cultural genealogy, each generation has a duty to improve upon the present and future environments. Thus, the two issues of protecting our built environment emerge. One, to preserve it. Two, to make the new environment a beautiful one.

Both of these issues are dependent upon the public being able to perceive important **concepts** in design, and to recognize the priceless parts of our architectural heritage. Many of our schools, and also our cities and towns, bear a silent witness to a general insensitivity. There is too much "visual illiteracy." Schools, with a potential for visual delight, are too often dismal, depressing fortresses, with curriculae to match.

Our cities could be paradigms of aesthetic sensitivity, but they seem to insist on being ugly grids full of unplanned frontage and automotive leftovers. They are our environment, and we live there and are affected by them. Change is so very difficult to bring about. But perhaps the best hope for change lies in raising the level of aesthetic maturity by becoming visually literate and raising a generation of visually literate children.

Like particles traveling at the speed of light, these mammoth efforts to enrich our built environment make the issue so vital that it is as if the past, present, and future are as one. The existing and future decisions must be based upon a visual literacy in design, theory, function and structure, and *cultural* heritage. The built environment cannot be ignored as being of paramount import.

This book is organized into very basic but important concepts about architecture. Concepts are what we learn most efficiently, and **concepts** are **behavior** determiners. So, if we want to change our personal and cultural behavior, understanding concepts is essential.

1.2.

The pollution of our visual environment can be explained conceptually—builders violate concepts and the results visually pollute the environment—and conceptualization is the only cure for the pollutants. What we are saying is that an ugly part of town or an ugly building *can* be explained in terms of form, value, shadow, reflection, texture, rhythm, site, color, variety, monotony, and a host of conceptual topics. *Figure 1.2* illustrates a need for caution in using concepts. It shows that the concept, "Variety may add interest to a design," may be *mis*-used, as too *much* variety leads to visual chaos. There are too many unrelated forms, textures, and colors. (The only unity comes from the artist's pen and its marks which bring a "sameness" not found at the actual site.)

Those who are unaware of unity in form will simply think this example to be "interesting," and accept it as all right. Imagine a whole generation of people who have given thought and attention to such conceptual issues, discussing whether the international style credo *"less is more and more is less"* is true, or whether the cry of the 1980s and beyond *"less is boring"* is closer to the fact. Reading this book, you will encounter hundreds of such vital issues.

This book outlines some of the most important concepts which are used by great architects. These concepts are taught at levels of perceptual maturity applicable to adults and children alike. The levels progress from one through seven as the concepts become progressively intertwined. While the concept is outlined to be understood by a six-year-old, it is at the same time discussed in such a way as to trigger challenges for even the most sophisticated designers. The human being does not fully perceive visual information until a concept is given to the brain to allow it to interpret what the eye receives.

"If I can get as much pleasure from touch, how much more beauty must be reached by sight. [Italic added] *Yet those who have eyes apparently see little.* The panorama of color and action is taken for granted. It is a great pity that the gift of sight is used as a convenience rather than as a means of adding beauty to life."—Helen Keller

In order to experience the role of a concept in visual thinking, ask some of your friends, "What color is a shadow?" You will be surprised. Most will answer "grey" or "black." Explain this **concept** to them: *"The color of a shadow is the color of the surface upon which it falls, but much darker in value with a hint of the complementary color in it."* Now, have them look at the yellow-green lawn outside, and the dark violet-green of the shadows on the grass. For the first time, they will begin to see color in shadows. As the result of conceptual understanding, we see the environment in a new and exciting way. This is why the teaching of visual concepts is so important. *The role of a concept is to allow the brain to interpret what the eye receives.* Without concepts we do not see.

This book is conceptualized for such cognitive interpretation, and the language is simplified because the concepts are a new challenge.

Visual Literacy. The aesthetic attack on our built environment is also based upon the fact that architecture, as a visual art, deals with sight. This visual perception is, after all, the ability to use imagery. It is the ability to perceive objects in space, to use and to comprehend graphic languages such as maps, blueprints, diagrams, drawings, models, and three-dimensional illusion. It is the ability to see and recognize visual order, texture, color, pattern, symbols, excellent craftsmanship, expression and beauty.

People who grasp these concepts will increase their visual literacy, their ability to think with imagery, and their cultural sensitivity. This sensitivity will ultimately provide the understanding and good sense to insist on a *quality* environment.

Literacy is the ability to read and write. *Visual* literacy is the ability to "read and write" visual images, as mentioned above. A student of architecture will be able to "read" the symbolism as seen on the Indian Stupa, or the linear declarations of a blueprint or the expression on a facade. Our twentieth-century culture has been said to be a "visually illiterate" civilization. If that is true, we should find symptoms of the disease all around us . . . and we do! In fact, a walk down almost any street will disclose many decisions made by visually illiterate leaders.

I.3.
St. Paul's Cathedral, London; Sir Christopher Wren, 1675-1710. The old view.

I.4.
The "new" view. Is it visual pollution?

I once met a man who sincerely felt that the ideal world would be a blacktopped one. "With only tar and asphalt to deal with," he argued, "we would have no grass to cut or flowers to water. There would be ample parking everywhere. There would be no mud, or dirt." If you are repulsed by this idea of efficiency, then you are beginning to see how visually literate people feel when choice gems of architecture and city plans are ruined at the rallying cry for efficiency. This is how they feel when a new building shows less empathy for the community than the building razed to provide its space. This experience is an example of the public "not missing" that which is not known. It is the symptom of visual illiteracy.

Many of our best architectural landmarks have been replaced by "the chain enterprise" idiom. This idiom is best described as standard, general, impersonal, generic, and plastic. It is a commercial identity image useful to homogenize all of America *in* that business image. Since most of this construction accommodates the automobile as the most important element, it tends to attack the personal, pedestrian environment. Even traditionally staid banks are now designed to replace service stations—shouting for visual attention—or are "parked" on corners in temporary structures.

1.5.

Architecture is closely related to and involved with many disciplines, including history, science, math, engineering, art and aesthetics, social studies, psychology, philosophy, computer science, and law. It is this wide divergence which makes architecture so effective in teaching people to become visual thinkers—one of the most prized skills of humanity. Aristotle said, "The soul never thinks without an image." Einstein said, "The words or the language as they are written and spoken, seem to play no role in my mechanism of thought. The physical entities which seem to serve as elements in thought are certain signs and more or less clear images which can be voluntarily reproduced and combined." It is this wonderful world of imagery that people enter into when they consider the subject of architecture.

Because people who become acquainted with this compilation of architectural concepts will develop a visual literacy, it is assumed they will develop a sensitive appreciation for the built environment, and make wise decisions in the future. They will insist on quality, on beauty and sensitivity.

In March 1981, another symptom of our visually illiterate culture challenged the public and educators of the nation. Few understood *educationally* what had happened, but the national test creators were embarrassed by a 17-year-old student from Florida, Daniel Lowen. The PSA Test on mathematics had the following question:

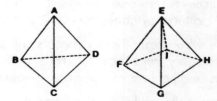

1.6.

In pyramids ABCD and EFGHI shown here *(fig. 1.6)*, all faces except base FGHI are equilateral triangles of equal size. If face ABC were placed on face EFG so that the vertices of the triangles coincide, how many exposed faces would the resulting solid have?

(A)5 (B)6 (C)7 (D)8 (E)9

Mr. Lowen answered *(A)5,* and with 250,000 other students was marked *wrong.* Mr. Lowen, evidently a visual thinker, felt that he was right. He built a model of the combined-pyramid form and proved his point. The professional mathematicians had fit into the left-hemispheric category of thinking. This approach is *verbal,* and tends to *label* in words and *count* in numbers. They simply counted pyramid sides, combined them and lost two, and concluded that only seven sides remained. If they had visualized, however, they would have noticed that when the equilateral pyramids were joined, two more faces were lost by becoming single planes on the solid. In fact, these pyramids could be hooked up alternately all day long and the new form would *still* have only five sides! The visual approach was more accurate than the verbal and counting approach, which is popularly called "basic" today. The key to our point is seen in Lowen's answer when asked about going to college on a mathematics scholarship. He said, "Math is all right, but I prefer literature." Of course! for he needs to nourish his imagery approach to problem solving on the basis of higher thinking skills. Many who see the drawings explaining Lowen's answer are unable to read the visual images of line, plane and form, and are not sure what was meant. They require a tangible, three-dimensional model, from which they can *count* the five sides.

Images precede and are *a priori* to words and numbers, and offer powerful and direct thinking power. Cognition is impossible without imagery.

What is being said and affirmed again and again is that the lay citizenry, mostly at the fourth grade level in perceptual ability, has very little idea of the power of thinking by the imagery process. As a result, the most image-laden courses of study— fine arts such as literature, poetry, art, architecture, music, dance, photography, and sculpture—are ignorantly labeled "frills," "non-basic," and "un-intellectual," thus unessential. This, like the math test question, exposes ignorance and left-brained myopia, and is a symptom of visual illiteracy.

Without overdoing this point, consider another example of problems which cannot be solved without visual imagery capabilities or training. Here is a problem given basic design students for many years: We have a child's building block with three holes *(fig. I.8),* all the same height. Design *one* hardwood block or peg which will fit *through* all three holes perfectly, shutting out the light, and sliding easily through each opening— whether the triangle, square, or circle—and come out the other side free and clear.

The "verbal/counter" types usually realize immediately that such a block or peg is impossible. After all, tradition has taught them repeatedly that a square peg cannot be driven through a round hole (especially if the hole and peg are the same maximum dimensions). They may even end the dialogue by saying, "Let's not waste time on this. Let's get back to *more basic* problems to solve."

Visual thinkers are not bothered much by such apparent ambiguity. As a result, they begin playing with alternatives, visually in their minds or on paper with drawings. These explorations may take forms like these images *(figs. I.9 and I.10).*

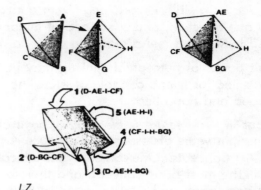

I.7.

I.8.

I.9.
The "fork approach," but it fails to pass all the way through the holes.

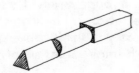

I.10.
The "all three" peg which fails because it, too, gets "caught" when pushed all the way through—the cylinder stopped by the triangle slot, and so on.

Eventually, the evidences and discoveries begin to unfold visually. For example, it is observed that a cylinder like the one in *figure I.11* can be put perfectly through both the square and the circular holes by simply turning it around. But how can it ever fill the demands of the triangle hole? Eventually, such visual solutions as *figures I.12 and I.13* present themselves.

This now leaves a "block" or "peg" with a **circle** as its base, a **triangle** at its midpoint one direction, and a **square** at midpoint in the third direction. (Some people may need to see and feel a model in order to realize this *is* one solution.)

While this power of perceptual thinking may be taught in any subject, those most naturally suited for it and capable of it are the fine arts, where imagery or imagination is developed and nourished.

The lessons in *Architecture Is Elementary* have an educational, developmental sequence based on eight years of research to produce *Art Is Elementary: Teaching Visual Thinking Through Art Concepts.*[1] One can easily see indications of such sequence by looking at some examples. The most basic concept, and therefore the first in the book, is that which develops perception and discrimination of **likenesses** and **differences.** If one perceives no differences, understanding is impossible. The second concept, on **order,** asks how your room is like other rooms in the "orderly" building. This concept builds on seeing differences and similarities. The **similes** the readers compose ask them to complete sentences such as "marching up the stairs is like _____." Creative thinking begins in these exercises. Another lesson asks, under **productive thinking,** "What are **all** of the ways these things are alike? Different?", so that the first concept must precede these in order for the new concepts to be perceived. A subsequent concept says that "if we do not perceive contrast, we perceive almost nothing." In sequence, likeness and difference is a key to understanding that concept. So you see that in this book, the sequence must logically begin at the beginning . . . with the perception of likeness and difference.

Time Lines. Another unique feature of this book's approach is that each level/activity has an accompanying visual time line to demonstrate the lesson's concept. Appendix A identifies the buildings and explains how, when, and where those buildings used the lesson concept. More often than not, each time line is in chronological order, though there are some exceptions.

Organization. The book is organized into levels of maturity, with concepts progressively intertwined from levels one through seven. These correlate with the maturity levels in *Art Is Elementary.*[2] For example, lesson 1/1 indicates the most elemental maturity level. Higher level thinking will improve as you think convergently and divergently and write similies and analogies. While the format begins simply enough for comprehension by five-

I.11

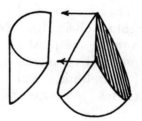

I.12.
Cut off one side of the cylinder, from the top diameter to the edge of the base.

I.13.
Cut off the other side in the same way.

1. Ivan E. Cornia, Charles B. Stubbs, Nathan B. Winters, *Art Is Elementary: Teaching Visual Thinking Through Art Concepts* (Salt Lake City: Gibbs M. Smith, Inc., 1983).

2. Ibid.

year-olds, potentially each concept is challenging to the most experienced designers and architects. You will understand why that is true as you progress through the text. The concepts are valuable to every generation.

History and Literacy. A large portion of the book deals with historic recognition of periods and styles, giving you a chance to assimilate your new knowledge of architectural concepts. Many libraries have slides and pictures of historic buildings available for practice in recognizing those periods and styles. Books on architecture are also an excellent source. Do not just "read" this book. You must do the suggested exercises to *experience* the concepts.

Architecture provides us shelter from the elements, privacy, beautiful spatial experiences, cities and towns, comfort, and humaneness, and it must be planned by humans to do those things.

CONCEPT

When objects look or feel just the same, we say they are alike. When they are not the same, we say they are different.

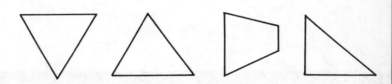

LESSON

The most basic concept in visual thinking is to perceive difference. Without this skill, all other concepts will be beyond grasp.

Are these shapes *(fig. 1.1)* **alike,** or are they **different?** (They are alike as circles, but different in size.)

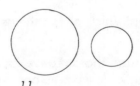

1.1

Compare scissors, books, balls, perhaps even people. Are these objects alike or are they different? Such a question appears to be simple. The fact is, some of us see much more in similarity and difference.

How is a pear like an apple? Can you **feel** if objects are alike or different?

Experiment by cutting out 3-inch circles or squares from fabric, sandpapers, plastics, etc., and put one sample in each hand while blindfolded. See if you can identify **alike** or **different** samples as you feel the surfaces.

Architecture, or buildings, may be alike or different. *See figures 1.2 and 1.3.* In creative, productive thinking, divergence begins with simple questions like these: How are they alike? How are they different? How is your house like these? How is it different?

1.2.
Eskimo igloo.

1.3.
Samoan fale (FAW-lay).

A

These questions can be answered in a simplistic, non-thinking way . . . or . . . on a profound, penetrating level, observing subtle, unusual comparisons.

Look at *figures 1.4 and 1.5.* How are they alike? How are they different? Many state capitol buildings in the United States are modeled after these two great cathedrals.

1.4.
**St. Paul's Cathedral, London;
Sir Christopher Wren,
1675- 1710.**

1.5.
**St. Peter's Basilica, Rome;
dome by Michelangelo,
facade by Maderna, 1537-1590.**

PRODUCTIVE THINKING

Divergent: What are all the ways the shapes in *figure 1.6* are alike? (Same color, both paper, same height or width, etc.)

What are all of the ways they are different? (One curves while the other is straight, angles, names, etc.)

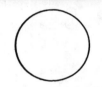

1.6.

Convergent: Try this one: Which of the things in *figure 1.7* is different from each of the others (has no "twin")?

Many creative researchers state that creative ideas often come from finding relationships using the process of **analogy.** A simile is one form of analogy.

Similes and Analogies: (Complete the statement.)

The little puppy is as frisky as _____.

(Some of the most beautiful examples occur when **likeness** is found in very unlike things.)

Make up a simile of your own which is more advanced than the puppy example.

(Complete the analogy.)

The roof is to the house as a _____ is to a _____.
(Mountain, cave)
(Sky, earth)
(Triangle, square)

1.7.
Which Sporthing doesn't belong?

(To complete an analogy, you must perceive the relationship between the choices.)

How is one house different from the other? *See figures 1.8 and 1.9.*

How is this Dutch Colonial home *(fig. 1.10)* different from this Georgian style home *(fig. 1.11)?*

1.8.
Colonial style.

1.9.
Mission style.

1.10.
Dutch Colonial style.

1.11.
Georgian style.

SUGGESTED ACTIVITIES

1. Using cut construction paper, crayons or pencils, origami, or clay, make shapes which are alike in some interesting ways. (Refer to origami paper-fold exercise in Activity 33 of *Art Is Elementary: Teaching Visual Thinking Through Art Concepts.*)

2. All trees look alike in some ways, and different in other ways. (Compare palm trees, pine trees, oak trees, etc.) How are these trees alike? How are they different? (Alike in having green leaves, trunks, branches, and roots. Different in size, height, shape—some are round, some triangular—, etc.)

Put about ½ teaspoon of wet watercolor, poster paint, ink, or stain on a sheet of paper. With a drinking straw placed close to the liquid, blow hard on the straw while wiggling it back and forth. Follow the droplets outward while blowing and continue to blow them until they run out. Notice that the lines created get smaller as they go out from the middle. Even people have a trunk, limbs, and "twigs" (fingers) like trees. Many living things are alike in this way. Many living things are also very different.

3. How are this building *(fig. 1.12)* and this seashell *(fig. 1.13)* alike? Find other buildings which look like something in nature.

4. Draw a house which has a tree beside or in front of it which is like the house in some way. (See *Art Is Elementary,* Activity 69).

1.12.

1.13.

5. Experiment with exercises in visual thinking, such as "visual analogy." (For ideas, refer to Miller Analogy Tests—1400 analogy questions by Turner, published by ARCO.)

Visual Analogy: Step one: All of these shapes *(fig. 1.14)* are alike in a special way. Can you see how? (They all point down.)

1.14.

Step two: None of these shapes *(fig. 1.15)* are alike in that special way. They are different. (None point down.)

1.15.

Step three: Which of these shapes *(fig. 1.16)* is like the first group? (Only **D** points down.)

1.16.

Draw or build an igloo. (For one source, see Lee J. Ames, *Draw 50 Buildings and Other Structures.* See also *Art Is Elementary,* Activities 46 and 84. Draw your own house beside the igloo.

Find two objects at home or out of doors which are alike. Then find two objects which are different.

From magazines or newspapers, cut out pictures of houses or buildings which are alike and different.

Take a walk and find things to compare.

1/2

When things are arranged in a line or circle, by shape, size, color, or in a group, it is said they are in order.

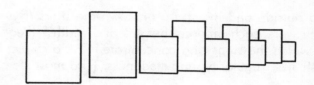

When we count 1, 2, 3, 4, 5 . . ., the numbers are in **order,** by putting in one more each time. If we say 1, 2, 5, 4 . . ., they would *not* be in order.

Look at *figure 2.1.* What line is next in order? The line in *figure 2.2* or the one in *figure 2.3?*

Order is, perhaps, the most essential **design** quality.

Put many objects on an overhead projector *(fig. 2.4)*, or on your table if you are studying alone. Are they in **order?** Can you put them in order? Do this as many times as you wish to demonstrate new ordering ideas. (Ordering may be accomplished by lining up the things, by size, by putting them into groups or categories such as wood, metal, plastic, or by color, etc.

Is your room **orderly?** *How* is it in order? Is your room ever *out* of order? How? (Not putting books back on the shelf, leaving scraps or waste paper around, etc.).

Look at the checkerboard in *figure 2.5.* Is it in order? Sometimes things are **too orderly** and they are monotonous to look at.

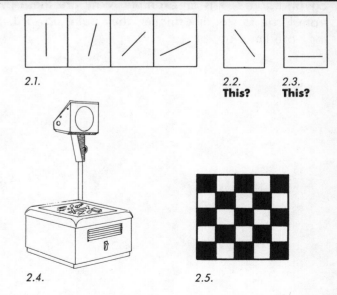

2.1.

2.2.
This?

2.3.
This?

2.4.

2.5.

B

Even your shoe has an order to it. For example, if your shoes lace, there are little holes for the laces, exactly side by side, up the front. If the holes were *not* in the side-by-side order, the shoe would lace crooked.

2.6.

Find other things which have an order to them. (Buttons and button holes, bicycle spokes and wheels, etc.)

When architects plan buildings, they put them in **order.**

Here is a way to feel order: Beat a nice, orderly, steady rhythm or play a metronome. Could someone **march** to this order? Beat an irregular, disorderly sequence and feel how someone would have to struggle to keep in time with it.

2.7.

Go outside and march up or down the stairs *(figure 2.7).* They are in **order.** What if they were each different heights and widths? (People would fall, would constantly have to watch the steps and concentrate.) The architect has planned our steps to be in order, with size, regularity, and steepness. (The *most* steep stair is a ladder.)

What are all of the ways it made you **feel** trying to march to disorder? Tell or list all the ways you felt marching up the stairs. Complete this simile: Marching up the stairs is like _____.

Figure 2.8 shows one of the step pyramids in Mexico. The earliest step pyramids are in Egypt; *figure 2.9* is an example. Why are these pyramids so **orderly?** (The steps go from large to steadily smaller, they point upward, the little steps are **like** the big steps, they are lined up, etc.)

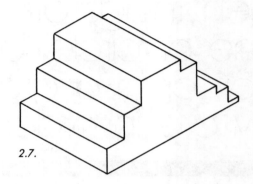

2.8.

2.9.

With a group of various sized and shaped blocks, make an orderly design, such as a building, using *all* of the blocks. *(See figure 2.10 for an example.)* Keep a special **order** to it. Try to create a building which is most **different** from other buildings.

Similes: (Completing these similes causes you to look for important relationships and feelings.)

Going up stairs which have no order is like _____. (Marching to disorderly beats, having only one roller skate, climbing over rocks, etc.)

Marching to order is like _____. (Breathing in and out, dancing, feeling ''in control,'' etc.)

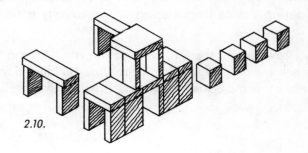

2.10.

SUGGESTED ACTIVITIES

Gather up groups of large cardboard boxes and make ''mini-environments'' with special **order.** Use them as tunnels, arrange from small openings to large, stack them like pyramids, form towers, etc.

At the end of this lesson (pp. 9-11) are a few pages that include a building facade and parts—doors, windows, lines, decoration, and columns. Glue the parts onto the facade in an orderly way. (The unusual but **orderly** solutions are best.)

ALTERNATE ACTIVITIES (MORE ADVANCED)

1. Order may be achieved by ordering things about a center object or space. *(See figure 2.11.)* (Activities 25 and 29 in *Art Is Elementary* relate to this.) Place geometric forms **around** a center tower, space, or other center. This center may be an **axis,** which must be arranged symmetrically.

2. Disorganized things may be ordered by clustering or grouping. Categorize various objects and cluster them into their own areas *(figure 2.12).* (See activity 16 in *Art Is Elementary.*)

Have someone you know put many objects into a sack. Use a great variety. Categorize the miscellaneous objects by material (metal, plastic, woods, etc.), colors, or size, and so on. You will grow from such divergent practice.

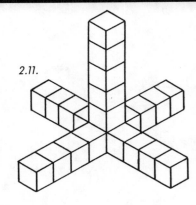

2.11.

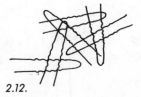

2.12.

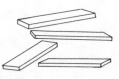

Next, rearrange the objects by various clustering methods. Though few shapes are alike, **proximity** is the common trait or relationship that can bind them into a unit. A visual ordering device to go along with proximity is usually necessary, such as **axis** *(figs. 2.13-2.15).*

3. Draw the Parthenon, and point arrows to the things which give **order** to this great Greek building *(fig. 2.16).* (Trace the building if you are unable to draw it.) Your memory is increased by **visual** practice like drawing, tracing, and observing.

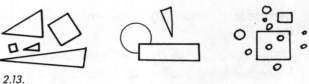

2.13.
Proximity

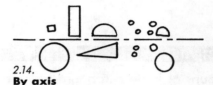

2.14.
By axis

2.15.
Around a center

2.16.
The Parthenon, Athens, Greece; Callicrates and Ictinus, 432 B.C.

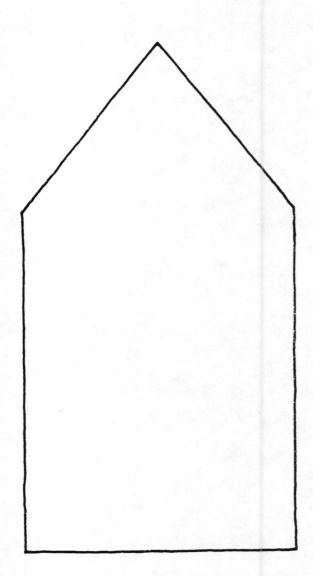

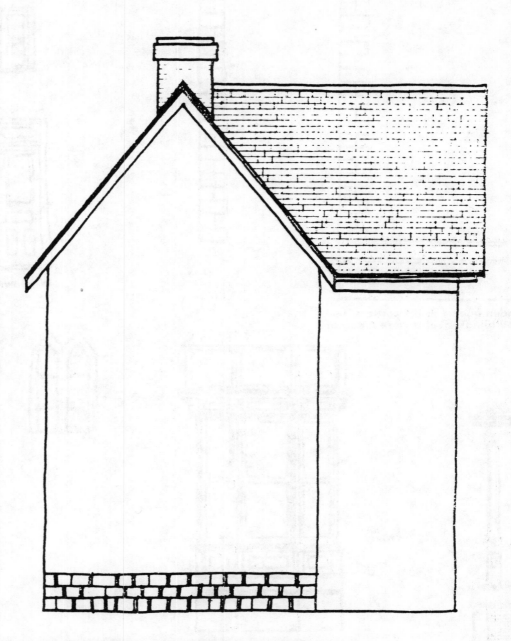

We start our Carpenter Gothic house with the tall, steeply pitched roof form of the Gothic Revival.

Our house sits on a stone foundation and has a wood-shingled roof and brick chimney.

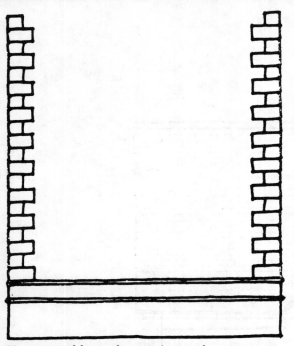

Next we add wooden quoins at the corners. In medieval Gothic buildings, quoins were made of stone.

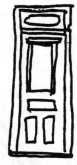

Windows and a door.

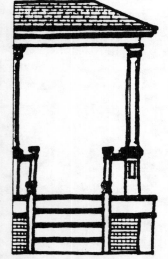

Add a wooden porch,

A slanted bay window adds character and charm.

The crowning touch of our Carpenter Gothic house is the ''gingerbread.'' The exterior walls are covered with novelty siding.

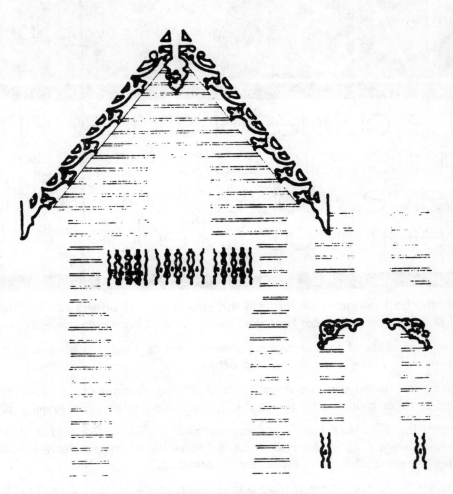

The Thomas Quayle House, Salt Lake City, Utah, built about 1888 in Carpenter Gothic style.

CONCEPT

The outlines of shapes and planes are called edges. Most perceptual relationships are determined by edges.

LESSON

Only the best designers understand the importance of **edges** to visual impact. Edges—as lines, contour, value contrast, texture, color and harmony—determine **relationships.**

When the edges of two or more planes or shapes meet, we often use a line to show that meeting place, even though no actual "line" as such exists there.

Edges occur when a plane stops; turns a corner; changes color, value or texture; or meets another plane, as in *figure 3.1.* (Planes are explained in Activity 10.)

What is the difference between these two planes *(figures 3.2 and 3.3)* and their "meeting edges"? Draw a line which indicates the connection of the edges. (Not all edges are crisp and clear, especially if **rounded.**)

Consider the place where a blackboard meets the wall. Is that really a line? Why? Why not?

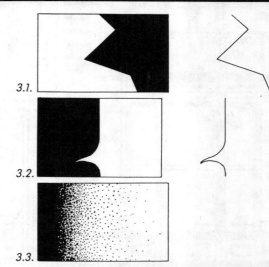

3.1.

3.2.

3.3.

Both planes change from dark to light, but in one the change is abrupt. In the other it is gradual.

C

A school yard has a fence around it. It is the "edge" of the playground. Where is the edge of the grass? (At the sidewalk, at the blacktop, or a wall?) What do we call the edge of a lake or the ocean? (The shore.)

Find and identify various concealed edges. Can you draw the edges of a ball? Of an egg?

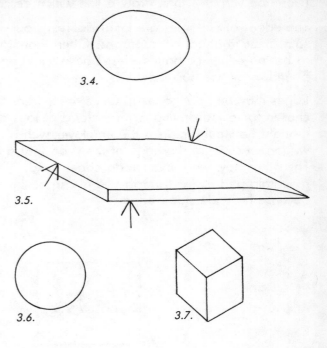

People once thought the world to be flat *(figure 3.5)*. They asked, "What happens when you get to the **edge?**" The answer was usually, "You **fall off**"—into space. It is very difficult to find the edge of a ball or sphere *(fig. 3.6)*. This is because there are no **sharp** turns or corners as are found on a cube.

Shape is the **description** of the edge or contour of an object, or its silhouette. It is seen as a line around the edge. *(Refer to figure 3.7.)*

Draw the edge/contour of at least 15 forms you observe in the room. *(Figures 3.8 and 3.9 are examples.)*

The architectural time line is an exercise in recognizing famous buildings by edge-silhouette. Begin to test your memory. Refer to the appendix for identification of buildings on the time line.

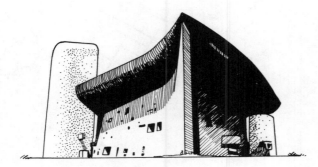

3.8.
Walls have edges, and so does the roof.

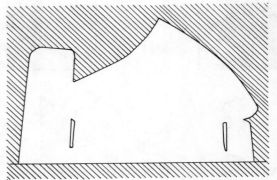

3.9.
The "background" has become the plane which meets the object's edge.

1. Concealed shapes—find the square.

Find linear edges of the shapes in *figures 3.10-3.18.* Next, color in the surrounding shapes, but leave *the* shape white.

2. The relationship of the edges in *figures 3.19, 3.20, 3.21* is:

(Describe verbally, then draw a line which describes each edge.)

The edges of countries are **boundaries.** Boundaries have shapes on maps and sometimes in aerial photographs. Often mountains, oceans, lakes, or rivers are selected to be the edges or boundaries. Does your room have a boundary? Where is the boundary of the building?

Edges may be "dangerous." Once there were two pioneer boys who were trying to be chosen for a job driving a wagonload of logs down from the mountains. One boy thought he would impress the employer with his great skill. He said, "I can drive a wagon so close to the edge of the road that a *mouse* would not have room to run by." The other boy, who understood edges, said, "I always keep my wagon as close to the mountain and as far from the edge as possible." The man hired the second boy because he understood edges.

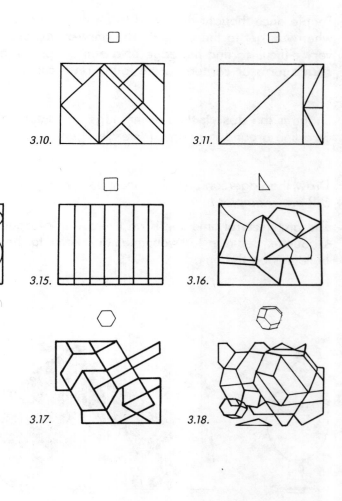

3.10.   3.11.

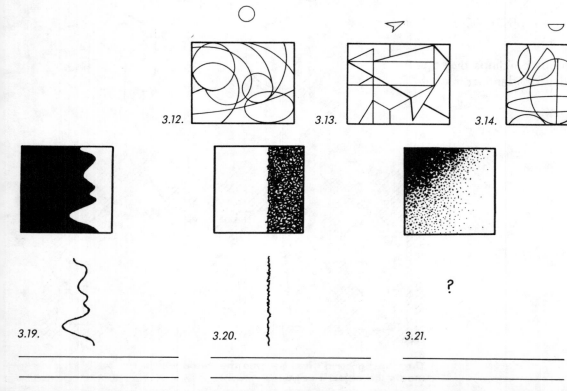

3.12.   3.13.   3.14.   3.15.   3.16.

3.17.   3.18.

3.19.   3.20.   3.21.   ?

CONCEPT

Four basic geometric shapes and forms, and their variations, are used by architects.

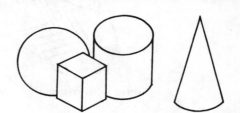

LESSON

All excellent designers are knowledgeable of basic shapes.

If you piled up many **squares** *(figure 4.1)*, they would be a _____. (Cube or box)

If you piled up many **circles** *(figure 4.2)*, they would be a _____. (Cylinder)

If you piled up circles which went from large to very small—even a point—*(figure 4.3)*, they would make a _____. (Cone)

If you piled up squares which went from large to very small *(figure 4.4)*, they would make a _____. (Pyramid)

If you lined up these triangles *(figure 4.5)*, they would look like a _____. (Roof, house, tent)

If you spin a circle *(figure 4.6)*, it is a _____. (Sphere or ball)

D

4.1.

4.2.

4.3.

4.4.

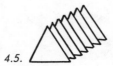

4.5.

4.6.

LESSON

How many new shapes or forms could you make by combining some of the forms named above? Draw some.

Figures 4.7 through 4.9 are some variations which come by changing the basic geometric forms.

4.7.
A cylinder with triangular notches cut out of it.

4.8.
Triangle (roof shape) form with a curved side. (Section from a cylinder.)

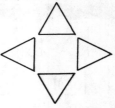

4.9.
Four triangles and an implied square.

PRODUCTIVE THINKING

Figure 4.10 is a square. By cutting off *one* portion and adding a portion of another basic shape, create a *new* shape.

What are all of the names for it that you can think of? (Names should relate to circles, squares, rectangles, triangles, line space, points, etc., rather than Judy, Billy, Fido, and so on.)

Similes and Analogies: Doughnuts are like _____. (Circles)

Crackers are like _____. (Squares)

So doughnuts are to circles as crackers are to _____. (Squares)

A pyramid is to a square as a cone is to a _____. (Circle)

(The relationship is that squares and circles, piled up from large to small, make those forms.)

Find a picture of a castle from a library book *(figure 4.11)*. How many forms can you identify? (Most authentic castles are from the Romanesque Period in history.)

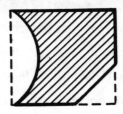

4.10.
Name: trisquarcle.

4.11.

Draw a castle which uses one or more of the four basic shapes. (Could you make a castle which does *not* use any of the four basic shapes?

Create your own new shape, name it, and color it.

Could your new shape be used for a house? Draw one.

Create a number of "piled up" shapes from cardboard, plastic, or any thick material. Try to pile up a series of new shapes and sketch the **form** they make. *Figures 4.12-4.24* are some shapes you can try. Can you "spin" their shapes to create new forms?

Visit a building which uses many of the forms discussed. Can you find any buildings or homes which use a "new" shape?

If you feel quite comfortable with shapes and forms, you might explore **double curvature** structures like the "hyperbolic paraboloid" which combines a parabola and a hyperbola by using only **straight** lines from a "folded" square frame (two triangles). *Figure 4.25* represents a hyperbolic paraboloid.

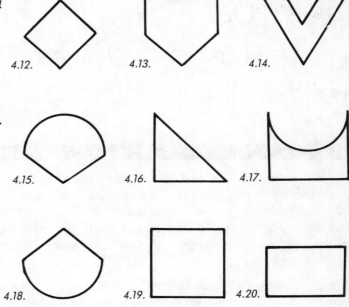

4.12. 4.13. 4.14.

4.15. 4.16. 4.17.

4.18. 4.19. 4.20.

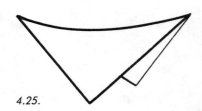

4.25.

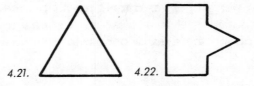

4.21. 4.22. 4.23.

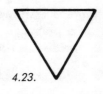

4.24.

CONCEPT

The size of things may be measured by comparing them with other things.

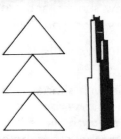

LESSON

As you remember, the first lesson emphasized looking for differences. Analogies and similes develop cognition of relationships. Architects have to judge the relative **sizes** of things. This helps them to understand weight (how heavy something is or appears to be), strength, and scale. The size of each part of a building or city is perceived relative to the sizes of other things around it. We know how large something is by comparing it to other objects.

Ancient Greek architects learned that if they put statues on buildings, they had to be **larger** than life. This was necessary because when the statue was looked at from down below, on the ground, it was so far away that it looked **small.**

The tent exercise: *Figure 5.1* shows a person next to a tent. The tent comes only to the arm. *Figure 5.2* show a person next to a larger tent. How do we know that this tent is larger? Our brain interprets by comparing the sizes of people to the relative tent sizes.

5.1.   5.2.

E

What are all of the **large** things you can think of? (List the answers.)

What are all of the **giant** things? (List them.)

What are all of the **tiny** things? (List them.)

Is a mouse tiny? Then is a mouse **tinier** than an ant? Is it tinier than an elephant?

Name all the things that would happen if cars were just the right size for children.
What if doorknobs were just right for three-year-olds? What if drinking fountains were
made just right for giants or basketball centers?

5.3.
Is this house large or small?

5.4.
Is this house large or small?

5.5.
Is this house large or small? How can you tell?

SUGGESTED ACTIVITIES

How are buildings out of scale with children? (Drinking fountains too tall, steps too
large, chairs too high, bathrooms too large, ceilings too high, doorknobs too high, light
switches too high, etc.)

Draw a giant's castle, giving visual **clues** as to how we know it is very large.

ALTERNATIVE ACTIVITIES

Make a **long** list of things out of scale for children. Identify which ones require
changing, given their locations, functions, and usage by children. Mail the lists to the
school board, governor, and the local institute of architects with your recommendations.

Make a drawing showing something very "out of scale."

1/6

Architecture (buildings and homes) has a big influence on each of us. It is our built environment.

Read "The Three Bears" to consider the architectural side of the story, with the house having doors and windows "just right," as well as the furnishings.

Read "The Three Little Pigs," noting the influence of architecture in this story . . . indeed, it is the characters' actual survival.

6.1.

Consider the basic needs of humans—food, shelter, clothing, safety,—and the decorative or art side of these needs (food aesthetically presented, shelter which is beautiful, and tools such as knives with decorated handles). It is important to realize that *art is the next basic need* after food, clothing and shelter, and it is often simultaneous with those basic needs. (Clothing, for example, can be **decorative,** and so can architecture.)

"Other" needs are met by architects too, such as bridges over rivers and canyons, or parks, or city plans.

6.2.

Read the introduction to this book again. It tells much about preserving and creating our **built environment.**

F

Divergent: Name all of the children's stories you can think of which have buildings in them. ("Hansel and Gretel," "Show White," "Cinderella," "Rapunzel," etc.)

What are all of the ways houses make you more comfortable? How many natural animal houses have you seen? (Beehives, hornet nests, tree holes, nests, etc.) Even animals enjoy "built environments."

Analogies: A den is to a bear as a _____ is to people.

A squirrel stores nuts in its hole like people store _____ in their _____.

Humans have communities, but fish live in _____.

A dome is to a Baroque building as a _____ is to a _____.

Why is a Samoan fale open to the air, while other homes have doors and windows? Design a fale with doors and windows, and draw the fale.

For Analysis: Visit the zoo. Look at habitats. Observe how architects control crowd movement and specialize buildings for people *and* animals. Make a diagram or plan of such movement.

Think about **city planning** and how bridges, streets, fences, freeways, parks, landscaping, rivers, and buildings affect those plans.

Go to an amusement park and see how architecture is necessary for fun.

Repetition is often used in planning buildings.

When we do something again and again, we are **repeating** it. One of the most used principles in architecture is **repetition.** Some of the things which can be used repetitively are size, shape, space, color, texture, and value. Architects may repeat doors, décor, windows, beams, columns, niches, arches, and modules (regular spacing of elements).

When repetition is used in music, it creates **rhythm** *(figure 7.1).* You can **hear** repetition. Listen to a record for repetition of sounds.

When repetition is used by architects to put things in order, it creates **visual rhythm.** *Figure 7.2* shows a building using things which repeat over and over again. Which parts of the building are being repeated?

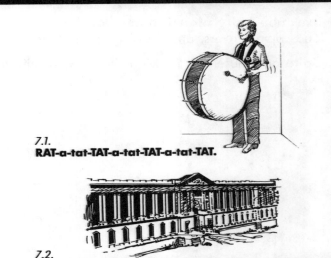

7.1.
RAT-a-tat-TAT-a-tat-TAT-a-tat-TAT.

7.2.
Louvre, Paris; Perrault, Le Vau, Le Brun, 1667-1670.

B

When an architect uses certain spaces over and over, a **module** is created. This is used in planning most homes and buildings *(figure 7.3)*. (See "Games" in Suggested Activities.)

Architects may **repeat** to save money, because everything "fits" and can be the same size from one room to the next, one building to the next.

Architects may repeat to speed construction time, because builders find it easier to do something over and over.

Architects may repeat things to give them a sense of **order.**

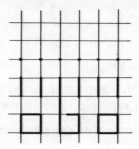

7.3.
Module plan.

PRODUCTIVE THINKING

Divergent: Here is a group of shapes *(figure 7.4)*. Arrange them by **repeating,** such as large/small, large/small, and so on. If you were to clap loudly for large squares and softly for small squares, you would create a repeated **sound** of rhythm. As in **order,** you can **feel** repetition.

Are there other ways to organize these shapes? *(See figures 7.5 and 7.6.)*

Convergent: Since each shape in *figure 7.7* is different, what is it that is repeated? (The notch.)

7.4. **SLOW** **FAST** **SLOW**

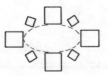

7.5.

7.6.

7.7.

What commonly played games are based on a module of repeated circular, rectangular, or square spaces or shapes? (Chess, monopoly, checkers, hop scotch, tic tac toe *(figure 7.8),* initials *(figure 7.9),* etc.)

Architects use modules too.

Play dominoes by lining them up in order (repeating small spaces), then tip them over and notice how visual repetition may have **movement in time,** like rhythm in music.

Suggestions for a basic design problem:

Below is a facade upon which you should be able to place columns, windows, and doors in variously **repeated** ways *(figures 7.10-7.15).* You can also cut out your own windows, doors, and columns, as well as draw your own.

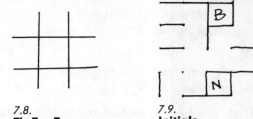

7.8.
Tic Tac Toe.

7.9.
Initials.

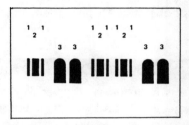

7.10.
Rhythm in a window arrangement. Can you make up a window rhythm?

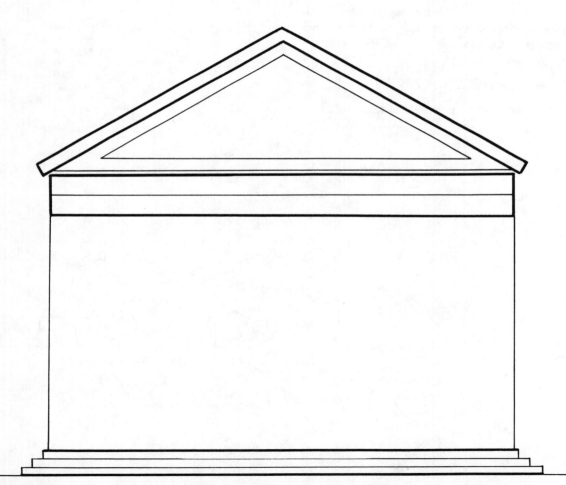

7.11.

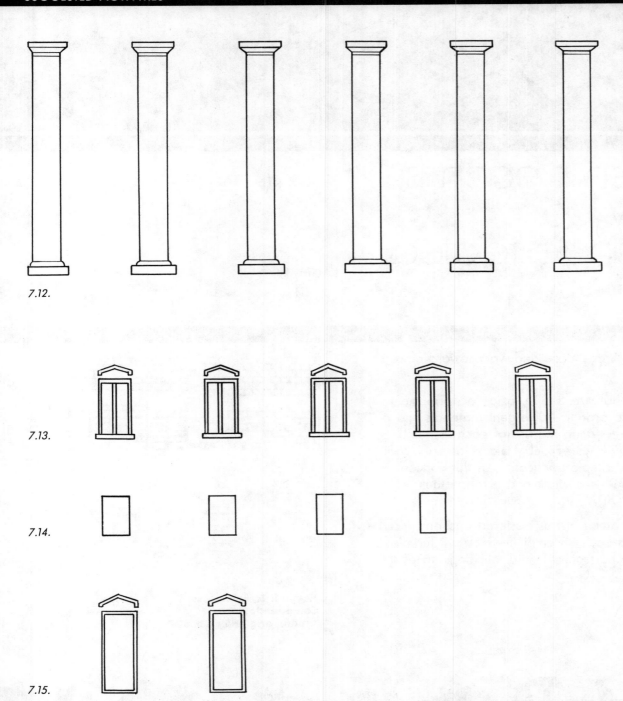

7.12.

7.13.

7.14.

7.15.

CONCEPT

Multiple forms, even if each is very different, may be arranged into a single related unit.

LESSON

Unity is a multiple-level concept. We begin with simple ideas and work toward more complex solutions.

All children love to work with blocks, no matter what size, shape, color, or form the blocks may be. This activity generates the ability to organize divergent materials into a cohesive unit—by stacking, grouping, piling, and repeating the use of each element. Frank Lloyd Wright often credited his childhood work with Froebel blocks as significant to his sense of form. In architecture itself, the most simple application of this concept is seen with the masons—either brick, block, or stone—who stack and arrange their elements into visual and constructive patterns *(fig. 8.1)*.

Figure 8.2 is a more complex example, where an architect has clustered and organized various forms into one single, related unit. Though each tower of the Horyu-ji Temple group is very different, the linear repetition of the horizontal frontal buildings unites the group into one single unit.

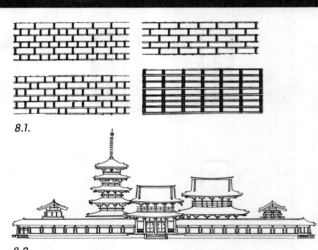

8.1.

8.2.
Horyu-ji Temple Compound, Nara, Japan; originally A.D. **607.**

G

Perceptual: Are the shapes in *figure 8.3* grouped or clustered? (No.) Are the shapes in *figure 8.4* clustered together? (Yes, into one unit.)

Can you think of anything which almost always "clusters together"? (Flowers, crystals, sedimentary rocks, leaves, cement lumps, etc.) Branches clustered into one unit are called a tree.

Analogy: If the opposite of white is black, what is the opposite of "one unit"?

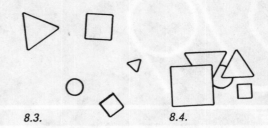

8.3.   8.4.

SUGGESTED ACTIVITIES

Build units or structures using many separate "blocks" or elements combined and **ordered** into one.

One can learn good design by purposely doing poor design. Make a design of shapes which do *not* cluster into one related unit. (It sometimes helps understanding to see the *absence* of the concept.

Explore social aspects of "clustering" into cohesive units by considering ant and bee colonies, and then condominiums, retirement communities, and so on. Can you think of three more social clusters?

Building human pyramids *(fig. 8.5)* is a way to cluster separate individuals into one related unit. Try it.

8.5.

2/9

Building blocks and other things can be arranged with various types of balance.

LESSON

Architects consider balance in their designs and make decisions early as to **symmetric** and **asymmetric** arrangements. Young children create such compositions by intuition, but they can learn to perceive balance more clearly and to understand their instincts. Architects traditionally have leaned toward symmetrical designs. Artists often call asymmetrical balance **informal** and symmetrical balance **formal.**

Balance scales are marvelous tools to demonstrate this concept. If none are available, you can make such a scale with a stick and a triangular block. Make a niche at the midpoint. *(See figure 9.1.)* (A 36-inch yardstick is usually too long for such a demonstration. Twelve to 18 inches is long enough.) Put various size and weight objects on the ''teeter totter.'' Begin with equal objects (identical) to show symmetrical or **formal balance.** Then move on to asymmetrical or **informal balance.** *(See figures 9.2 through 9.5.)*

C

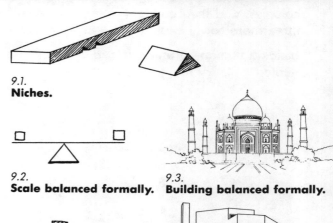

9.1.
Niches.

9.2.
Scale balanced formally.

9.3.
Building balanced formally.

9.4.
Scale balanced informally.

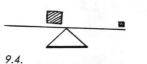

9.5.
Building balanced informally.

Swings and rides are based on balance, as is bicycle riding. Balance can be **felt** as easily as it can be seen *(fig. 9.6)*.

Stand on one leg.

Explore teeter totters.

Balance beams and boards.

Practice simple gymnastic movements.

9.6.

PRODUCTIVE THINKING

Convergent Analysis: Transfer the feeling of balance into perceiving balance in architecture. Find pictures from magazines or books or art prints that represent different kinds of balance and unbalance. Ask yourself these questions: "Is this building balanced? Is it balanced equally or unequally? Is it the same on each side, or different?" It is important to recognize that a symmetrical building may appear to be asymmetrical if seen from certain angles or viewpoints.

9.7.
Balanced? (Yes.) Equally? (Yes—same on both sides. It has symmetrical balance.)

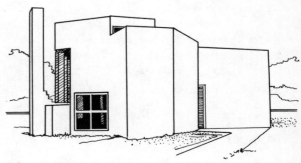

9.8.
Balanced? (Yes.) Equally? (No. It has asymmetrical balance.)

Much of the lesson has been "activity" oriented. For further practice, go through magazines and make tracings of buildings. Label each as formal, informal, or *un*balanced, if any are found.

A tug-of-war can be a fun exercise in balance. You might also try a "one on one" tug, working with a partner to create informal balance compositions by balancing one another, as in *figure 9.9.*

9.9.

Find examples of balance in athletics to compare with balance in architecture *(fig. 9.10).*

To further develop the idea of balance, consider balance in society, such as balance of payments, balance of living standards, balance of races, and so on.

9.10.

CONCEPT

When things are repeated in regular or irregular sequence, pattern is created.

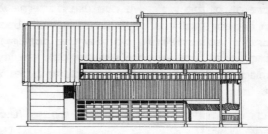

LESSON

Things which may be repeated in an architectural design are line, color, texture, form and shape, and value (darkness). For examples, *see figures 10.1 through 10.5.*

Patterns may be carefully planned, or accidental or random. Patterns involve **repetition** (using something over and over again.) Patterns may "overlay" other patterns (in design this is called counterpoint), as in *figure 10.6.*

10.1. LINE:

Regular   **Irregular**

10.2. **COLOR:**

Regular   **Irregular**

10.3. **TEXTURE:**

Regular   **Irregular**

10.4. **FORM:**

Regular   **Irregular**

10.5. **VALUE:**

Regular   **Irregular**

10.6. **Counterpoint**

A

What is the difference between a **line** *(fig. 10.7) and a* **shape** *(fig. 10.8)? Are there any different shapes in your room? Where? Are lines always needed to make shapes?* (No.) Look at your clothing. Can you find any lines or shapes on them? Look around carefully to see any **shapes** which are repeated over and over again. Can you find any **lines** which are repeated? What is the result called when a shape is repeated again and again? (Pattern.) There is pattern in some shirts, blouses, and dresses. Where can pattern be seen in your room? (Window panes, book shelf, ceiling tiles, etc.) What would clothes look like if it were against the law to use pattern?

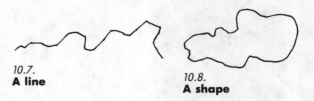

10.7.
A line

10.8.
A shape

What are all of the ways we can use pattern? Are patterns used in nature? Look at the seeds in a pear that has been sliced in half. Look at the bottom of a turtle. Look at a zebra and a leopard. How do they use pattern? The zebra's stripes look like shadows of grass and limbs. The leopard's spots look like leaf shadows and spots of sunlight. Camouflage makes it easy for animals to hide. What other animal or insect patterns can you think of?

Architects use pattern in many ways. *Figure 10.9* is a plan using a **grid.** Is anything repeated? What?

How does the skyscraper in *figure 10.10* use pattern? What is the pattern you see?

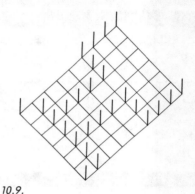

10.9.

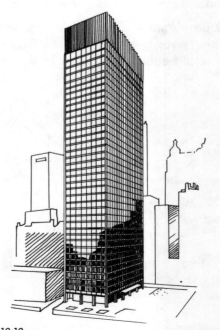

10.10.
Seagram Building, New York City; Ludwig Mies van der Rohe, 1956-1958.

What is repeated in the little town near Cisternino, Italy *(fig. 10.11)?* (The cone-shaped roofs, windows, doors, etc.)

The Elizabethan home in *figure 10.12* is typical in England. In what ways does it have pattern?

Figure 10.13 is a close-up of a wall. Describe its pattern.

10.11.
Rural community, Trulli, near Cisternino, Italy.

10.12.

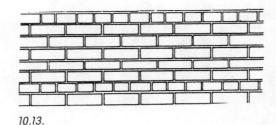

10.13.

SUGGESTED ACTIVITIES

What is the relationship of **pattern** to **rhythm?** (Both based on repetition.) Using that relationship, create an analogy. For example, "Pattern is to rhythm as texture is to beat." There are many analogies. Can you think of one?

Weave colored paper strips, repeating colors and the resulting rectangular pattern. (See Activity 54 in *Art Is Elementary.*)

Carve potatoes which have been cut in half, and make a shape on the surface. Dip the potatoes into tempera and make a potato-print pattern. (Place tempera, not too watery, in a paper plate *on top of* a napkin which will act as a stamp pad.) This can also be done with an apple. Textile paint may be used instead of tempera to print a piece of cloth or a T-shirt.

Figure 10.14 is a pattern of animals. Can you find a way to draw **straight lines** through the pattern from the bottom to the top, using only two straight lines? (Don't touch any animals or trouble will be yours!)

Sometimes it is difficult to find a pattern. See if you can find hidden shapes in *figures 10.15 through 10.18.*

Cut out ''brick-shaped'' pieces of paper. Create patterns for brick laying. *(Figure 10.19 is one example.)*

10.14.

10.15.
Can you find this shape . . .

10.16.
In this pattern?

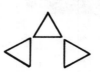

10.17.
How about this one?

10.18.
In this?

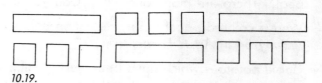

10.19.

2/11

CONCEPT

Variations in the sizes of people, objects, and buildings can be determined by eye, or by measuring with rulers or other objects.

LESSON

(This lesson will ultimately lead to an understanding of the topics of **scale** and **proportion.**)

What is the tallest animal? Which is the shortest animal? Who is the tallest person you know? Which is the tallest building in your city? How do you *know* it is the tallest? (By comparing it, by measuring it or counting stories, etc.) What is the tallest building in the world? *(See fig. 11.1.)* Which buildings are *nearly* as tall?

Which is the shortest building in the world? What is the **limit** to being the shortest? (People have to walk around in them.) Earth-sheltered buildings often appear short because they are **below** the surface. If a building is smaller than people, will it be useful?

E

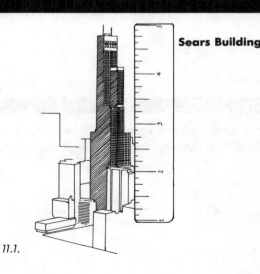

Sears Building

11.1.

Frank Lloyd Wright once designed a mile-high building (the last example on the time line for this lesson). Explain how high that is by **comparing** it to other things. (It would be like putting _____ Sears Buildings on top of each other. It would be like _____ people standing on each other's shoulders, etc.)

PRODUCTIVE THINKING

What are all of the small or tiny things on a building? What are all of the large things you might find on a building? *(See figures 11.2 and 11.3.)*

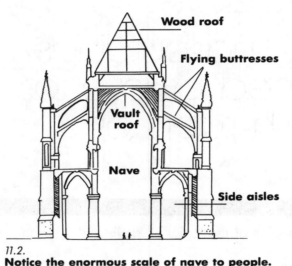

Wood roof

Flying buttresses

Vault roof

Nave

Side aisles

11.2.
Notice the enormous scale of nave to people.

11.3.
Scale of the Great Pyramid of Khufu compared to some of the buildings today, such as the Sears Tower.

SUGGESTED ACTIVITY

Draw a city and make it **appear** to be small by putting something unusual in the picture which is normally "small" but is now "giant." *(Figure 11.4 is one example.)*

11.4.

2/12

An architectural composition may have one or more shapes, colors, textures, lines, or themes that relate parts to one another.

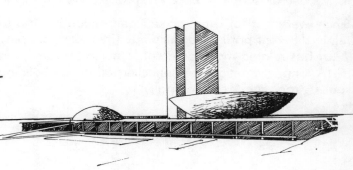

If a path or a road needs to go across a canyon which is very deep, something needs to be built to connect the two walls of the canyon. This connector is called a _____ (fig. 12.1). What are all the materials from which a bridge could be made?

How many **relations** (relatives) do you have? How and why are you **related?** (Same family, we look alike, etc.)

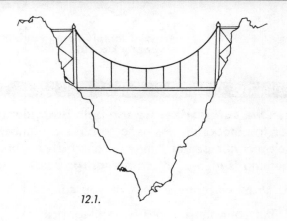

12.1.

G

When we make **designs,** we sometimes need to **relate** the parts to each other with "bridges" or transitions of one kind or another. If we have these two shapes in our design *(fig. 12.2.),* they look quite isolated, lonely, and like "something else is needed." What can we do to make these two shapes less lonely by relating them in some way? How could we give them some relations? (Similar shapes, lines, color, etc.)

If we use related shapes, we could make a bridge in the design to tie the two together *(fig. 12.3).*

If we use something else to make more "family relations," this would help relate them to the overall shape *(fig. 12.4).* (Make a connecting triangle similar to the one shown.)

Since every part of a design or composition is important, how do you think architects relate different parts of a building? (By colors, shapes, lines, etc.) This architect *(fig. 12.5)* has related many different forms in his family group by one clever thing. What is it? (A long, rhythmic line connecting all of the buildings—using similar proportion, spaces, roof line, and materials.)

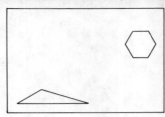

12.2.

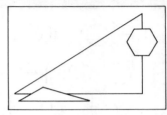

12.3.

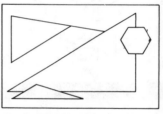

12.4.

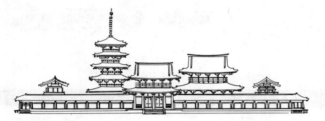

12.5.
Horyu-ji Temple Compound, Nara, Japan; originally A.D. 607.

PRODUCTIVE THINKING

When we **categorize,** we use both divergent and convergent thinking. For example, in order to categorize, we need to have a number of things to put into categories. To develop a number of things is called **diverging.** When we choose which category something is in, we are **converging.** Below are some games to try.

I. A. Draw as many shapes as you can.

   B. Put your shapes into two categories.

      1. Shapes with circles or curves *(see fig. 12.6).*

      2. Shapes with straight lines *(fig. 12.7).*

  How are the two shapes in *figure 12.8* related? How are they different?

12.6.

12.7.

12.8.

II. A. Create a "family" graph (relationships may be **visual** or **verbal**). *Figure 12.9* is a warm-up to creating a graph of relationships.

B. Next, try to add more to the architectural family graph or chart in *(fig. 12.10)*.

C. Try completing this chart *(fig. 12.11)*, then make up some of your own.

Class Name	Red		Yellow	
Flower	(Rose)		(Dandelion)	
Food	(Apple)		(Pear)	

12.9.

Class Name	Food	Car	Sleep	Study
Room				
Furniture				

12.11.

Class Name	Triangle		Circle	
Building Part	(Roof)		(Window)	
Tree	(Pine)		(Apple)	

12.10.

Use this story to practice seeing family or relationship: Once some people decided to take a long hike into the woods. They saw many interesting things along the way. As they came around a dark pathway under the trees, they saw a clearing with some tree stumps. Just as they got to the clearing, out from behind the stumps jumped some strange little creatures. "Boo!" they shouted. "We can't find our family. We look too much **alike.** Help us, will you? Please?" The people and gobies sat down together and looked at each other. The people tried to put the gobies into their correct families. Here are some of those gobies *(fig. 12.12)*. Can you find their differences and put them into **order** in their families? (Put a circle around one family, a box or square around another, and a line through the third.)

What are all of the ways this leaf structure *(fig. 12.13)* is like this high altitude map of a city *(fig. 12.14)*? (Things move along the arteries or veins, there are major arteries and minor, there are subdivisions, etc.)

12.12.

 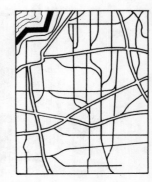

12.13.   12.14.

Figure 12.15 has two shapes. What are all of the ways they are alike? (One is a banana, the other is an orange—they are both fruit; both have curves; both on same sheet, etc.) What are all of the ways they are different? (One is long, the other short and compact; one is to the left, the other to the right; one is pointing, the other is "just there"; one bleeds off the border, the other is completely inside the border.)

The ways they are **alike** is how they are related. If we wanted to make them *more* related, what might be done to change the design? *(See fig. 12.16.)*

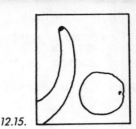

12.15.

12.16.

Figure 12.17 shows three buildings. **Relate** them by changing or adding to them. The Romanesque cathedral at Hildesheim, Germany, *(fig. 12.18)* uses these very forms related with a nave and a few other blocklike forms, such as pyramids, cubes, cones and planes.

Try cutting out five shapes, and move them around until they relate to each other by touching (proximity), overlapping, similarity, or by being subdivided into parts *(fig. 12.19)*.

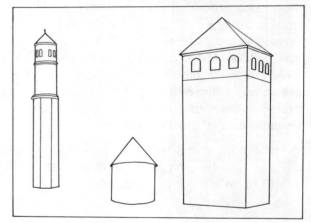

12.17.

12.18.
Abbey Church of St. Michael, Hildesheim, Germany; 1001-1031.

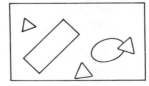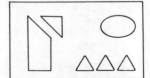

12.19.

3/13

Contrast may be used to create an area of emphasis.

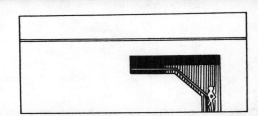

Architects use contrast to draw attention to an entry, an exit *(fig. 13.1)*, a particular room, or something of importance. When Frank Lloyd Wright was asked to design the little Morris Shop in San Francisco, California, he was shown the location and other stores and signs up and down the street. His problem was to make people **notice** the Morris Shop. As he looked up and down the street, many signs and neon lights "shouted" for attention. Using **contrast,** Wright decided to have a "quiet" store. The only sign would be a little plaque by the entry: "This is the Morris Gift Shop." Can you find the entry *(fig. 13.2)*? How is it different from the other stores? (No big sign, no windows full of things to sell, line leading to the front door, etc.) Using contrast, he solved the problem. Everyone notices this simple entrance, while the visually "noisy" buildings go largely unnoticed.

13.1.

13.2.
Morris Shop (now the Helga Howie Boutique), San Francisco; Frank Lloyd Wright, 1949.

A

Artists talk about the "area of emphasis" as either a "center of interest" or a "focal point." When we want a center of attention, contrast may be used very effectively. For example, the graffiti in *figure 13.3* has no definite center of interest. Now draw in another shape—one slightly different in size—and see how it makes your eyes want to keep looking there. It is now the area of emphasis because it contrasts with the others in size and shape. This is a "secret" or tool which architects use to make us look in particular places or move in certain directions. *(See fig. 13.4.)*

13.3.

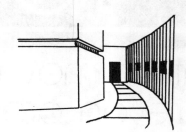

13.4.

PRODUCTIVE THINKING

Select a group of objects *(fig. 13.5)*. Arrange them so that one object attracts most of your immediate attention.

Now arrange the objects so that another one is the center of emphasis. Continue rearranging until every object has been the focal point.

What are all of the places in your home which require special attention so as to be easy to find? (Entrance, kitchen, bathroom, first aid cabinet, fire extinguisher, etc.)

Figure 13.6 is an International style home. How can you use contrasting shape, value (darkness), color, or texture to emphasize the front door? Some examples are found in *figure 13.7*.

The "family" of relationships is **lines** and rectangles. *(See fig. 13.7.)* The **contrast** should be with those family relationships. Remember that too much contrast may destroy the harmony and unity.

13.5.

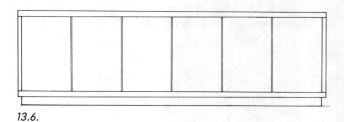

13.6.

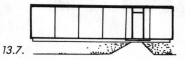

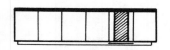
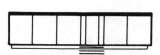

13.7.

Here is a room *(fig. 13.8)*. Design the walls, carpet, and furnishings so that contrasting color makes one part of the room the point of emphasis. *See figure 13.9* for one room design. (You may make paper cutouts to move around or redraw the room and its furnishings in several different arrangements.) Remember, it is very important that you stop reading this text and take time to do these exercises.

Take a walk around your house or another building, and find areas of contrast which demand your attention. Analyze what the contrast is, how it is contrasted, and how it could be done in other ways.

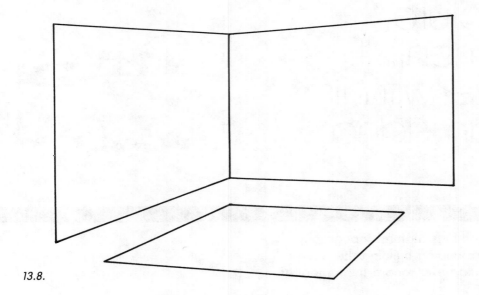

13.8.

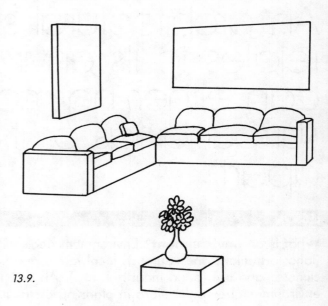

13.9.

3/14

CONCEPT

An architectural structure relates to its environment. It can either harmonize with its surroundings or it can stand apart.

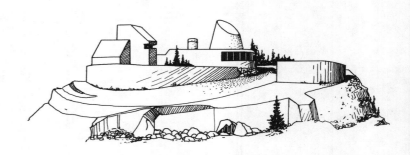

LESSON

What is an **environment?** Environment deals with many things: natural topography (land formations and contour), local fauna and flora, surrounding building themes, climate, land use (park, industrial, etc.). An architect should never ignore the important environmental considerations in planning a structure.

PRODUCTIVE THINKING

Divergent (Verbal): 1. How many environments can you think of? (Mountains, plains, cities, seacoast, industrial, park, etc.)

2. What type of building would be appropriate in each of those settings? The unity a building achieves within its environment depends on how well the structure "fits in" with its environment. For example, there would be little unity between a log cabin and a setting in New York City's Manhattan section, or a 110-story skyscraper in Yellowstone National Park.

G

Analogy: Create an **analogy** like the ones below.

Log cabins are to New York City as skyscrapers are to Yellowstone National Park. (Inappropriate)

Tree frogs are to hot deserts as horned toads are to the rain forests.

Igloos are to the equator as grass huts are to the North Pole.

Violins are to a rock band as electric guitars are to a symphony orchestra.

What are the ways structures may conflict with their environment? (Building materials, functional design, climate, topography, existing themes, landscape.)

Considering architecture in relationship to its environment can create **unity**—a condition of harmony where design corresponds with function and fits with its surroundings. *(See fig. 14.1.)* Buildings which express unity possess a cooperative spirit. They fit.

A sample analogy of things that fit might be:

Adobe is to a pueblo dwelling as paper is to a wasp nest. (The analysis is that both are functional, both use native materials, and both have colors which merge them with nature.)

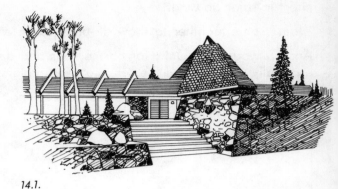

14.1.

Divergent (Verbal): Draw as many harmonious housing structures from nature as you can.

Design a structure to fit into an environment for real and imaginary animals or people. (Consider materials, structure, function, climate, socialization.)

Convergent: Build several models with boxes made of foam core or construction board. A variety of forms will be needed. *(See figs. 14.2 through 14.7.)*

14.2.

Taping tabs
Folds
14.3.

14.4.
Cylinders

Taping tabs
14.5.
Single faced corregated board

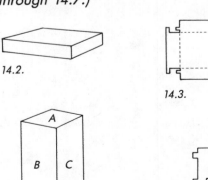

14.6.

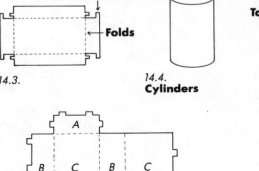

14.7.

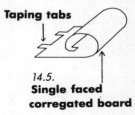

Divergent: After the models are constructed, place them in an "environment," such as a sandbox, and "berm" some to demonstrate the unifying effect of topography *(fig. 14.8)*. (Berm means to pile up or build up earth around a form. It is used with great effect in solar housing.)

"Jam" some together to show dis-unity as an environment *(fig. 14.9)*.

Analyze your community for harmonious and disharmonious relationships. Look especially at styles and themes, materials, colors, textures, and functions.

Finally, arrange a pleasant, harmonious setting. Use dried weeds and hills to landscape.

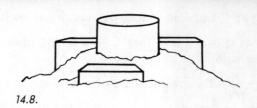

14.8.

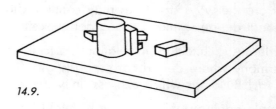

14.9.

CONCEPT

Walls, ceilings, floors, and other flat surfaces are called planes.

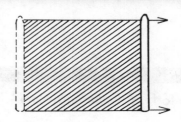

LESSON

A piece of chalk can draw a line. If we "drag" that line, it marks a **plane** *(fig. 15.1)*.

If you pull down a blind, it makes a plane.

Shape is a plane's **identity.** Planes may be named or identified as circular, triangular, or rectangular, or **combinations** of those shapes *(fig. 15.2)*.

Architects use planes to plan buildings and houses. The **overhead plane** may be the roof or ceiling. The **wall planes** are the walls in our homes *(fig. 15.3)*. (Doors and windows are part of the wall planes.)

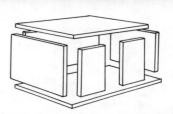

15.1.
Plane

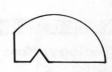

15.2.

15.3.

H

The **base planes** are the ground or floor *(fig. 15.4)*.

Any of the planes may be sloped, raised, lowered, or changed in some way to make them interesting *(fig. 15.5)*.

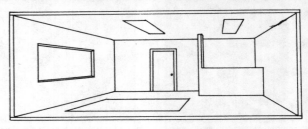

15.4.

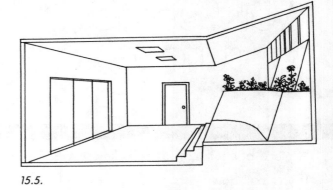

15.5.

PRODUCTIVE THINKING

Analogy: Plane is to form (volume) as line is to shape. (Boundary and descriptive relationship.)

Planes are used to enclose **volume** (form) as **lines** are often used to outline **shape.** (They are boundary determiners.)

Because architecture is a visual art dealing in three-dimensional volumes of form and space, planes are extremely important.

The visual properties of the planes determine the qualities of the volume and space they enclose. Planes may be folded, twisted, and penetrated *(fig. 15.6)*.

Try this analogy:

A folded plane is to a hallway as rhythm is to _____ (pattern, movement, etc.) *(fig. 15.7)*.

15.6.
Folded plane with penetrating plane.

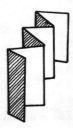

15.7.

Place a ground plane on your table. (You may use cardboard for such planes.) Using four sheets of stiff paper, create some interesting wall planes. (If folded, the planes will stand up.)

Put a ceiling plane on top of your walls, creating a room *(fig. 15.8)*.

Could you make windows or doors in your wall planes? (Yes, with scissors, or by folding so that openings are left.) (See Lesson 4/25—International Style and the New Brutalism— for architects' application of this concept.)

What are the relationships and differences between airplanes *(fig. 15.9)*, building planes *(fig. 15.6)*, and the plains *(fig. 15.11)*)?

Consider ceiling planes as sky, clouds, canopies, roofs, etc.

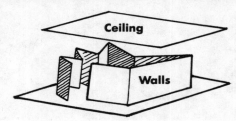

15.8.

Wall planes in the models are more rigid if stiff paper or cardboard is used, and if tabs are used to glue them to the ground at the bases.

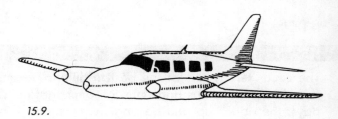

15.9.

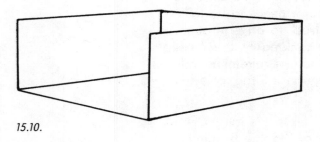

15.10.

15.11.

LEVEL / ACTIVITY

3/16

The function of a building influences its form.

The circus tent is one of the best traditional examples of architectural form and function *(fig. 16.1)*. The circus had unusual functional needs. It had to arrive in town, stay a few days, then pack up and be on its way again. It needed to keep the rain and sun off large groups of people who came to see the circus. The tent could be put up quickly and taken down and transported just as easily. It was high enough for the trapeze artists; it was large and colorful, and it could be packed up and put into trucks or railroad cars for moving.

16.1.

If a large truck needs to pull into a garage to have its motor repaired, the size of the truck determines part of the building's function *(fig. 16.2)*. The form needs to be tall enough for a large truck and have a door large enough for a truck to drive through. It may require a pit for workers to be able to get underneath the truck easily. It will need excellent ventilation with air fans, openings, and outlets. All of these requirements will affect the look of the building, just as the needs of the circus require a large, colorful tent.

Louis Sullivan was a great architect who lived in Chicago in the 1800s. He taught Frank Lloyd Wright as a young architect. He said, "Form follows function." Some buildings meet their function, but their form may remain ugly and unresponsive.

16.2.

B

How many examples of function problems can you think of? For example, a pencil sharpener without a basket to catch shavings *(fig. 16.3)*, a wastebasket without a bottom on it, a toothbrush with no bristles, a house with no roof.

Do you remember the story of ''The Three Bears''? Some of the things Goldilocks found were not very functional, but others were ''just right.'' Can you remember which things were just right? Those are the functional things for her size and her needs.

Sometimes the materials an object is made with influence how it looks. Would iron pillows be very nice to sleep on? They would last a long time and not wear out. Would wooden windows be very functional? Why not?

How has the **form** of the teacher's chair been influenced by its **function** *(fig. 16.4)*? How has this plane's form been influenced by its function *(fig. 16.5)*?

How has this building's form been affected by its function *(fig. 16.6)*? (World's largest building for world's largest retailer; offices, power, etc.) Is it beautiful? It was a unique designer's idea to use a ''bundle'' of rectangular tubes as a structure. They strengthen each other.

How has the building in *figure 16.7* been influenced by its function?

The flying buttresses of a Gothic cathedral look decorative, but they are functional parts that help control the outward thrust of the ceiling vaults.

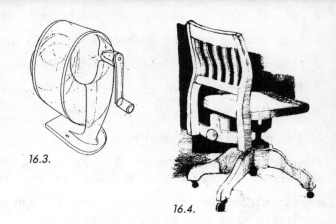

16.3.

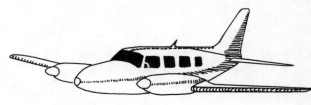

16.4.

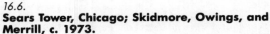

16.5.

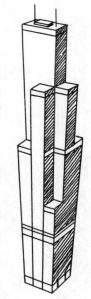

16.6.
Sears Tower, Chicago; Skidmore, Owings, and Merrill, c. 1973.

16.7.

If you can complete these **analogies** logically, you understand the concept.

1. Function is to form as fire/heat is to _____. (Chimney, firebrick, etc.)

2. How it *looks* and how you *use* it are the same as its _____. (Form)

3. Form is to function as _____ is to lawn sprinkler *(fig. 16.8)*. (Hose, pipe, spout)

4. Form is to function as _____ is to _____.

Make up some new analogies.

Divergent: Design a house which has a nice relationship of function and form. It should ''work'' and should ''look like'' its work. *(See fig. 16.9 for an example).*

Redesign something you use every day, but ignore how you use it. Do not worry about relating its form or its function to the design.

16.8.

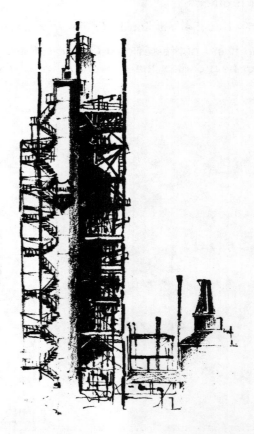

16.9.

Nature is a model for architectural forms and shapes which are variations of the cone, cube, cylinder, sphere, and pyramid. Nature is also a model for architectural forms which are not so geometric (Euclidean).

Snowflake

Rose window

LESSON

When we speak of nature, we mean the things which are part of the world which humans have not made. We mean such things as the sun and sky, the leaves, seashells, crystals, and rocks.

By learning to look closely at small things, and at a distance from large things, we get ideas for shapes, color, texture, and form. If a snowflake should fall on your sleeve you

c

could look at it with a magnifying glass. If it were a flat flake, you would see that each flake is **different,** yet all are **alike** in many ways *(fig. 17.1)*. For example, they appear "starlike" and have six points. They are symmetrical—the same around the center—and are hexagonal in shape. Yet, with such similarities, each is very different. They bear a striking resemblance to rose windows in Gothic cathedrals.

Look how similar the seashell *(fig. 17.2)* is to the spiral ziggurat Thanksgiving Square Chapel in Dallas, Texas *(figs. 17.3 through 17.5)*. The chapel was designed by Philip Johnson and John Burgee.

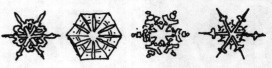

17.1.

17.2.

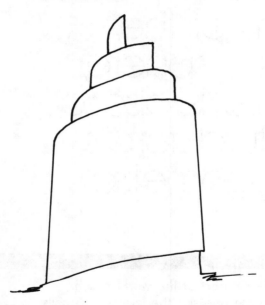

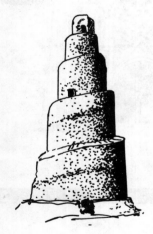

17.3.
Spiral minaret of Great Mosque of Samarra, Iraq,
A.D. **848-852.**

17.4.
Thanksgiving Square Chapel, Dallas; Philip Johnson and John Burgee, 1977.

17.5.
Thanksgiving Square Chapel interior, looking up.

Buckminster Fuller used such natural ideas. He designed a structure called the **geodesic dome.** Here are some pictures of alveoli cells *(fig. 17.6).* Notice how similar they are to Fuller's dome *(fig. 17.7).* He had to arrange his basic shapes to connect easily and form a rounded surface, even though he used only straight building materials.

Look how similar the seashell *(fig. 17.8)* is to the minaret *(fig. 17.9).*

The Opera House in Sydney, Australia *(fig. 17.10)*, sports some similar shell shapes *(fig. 17.11)* in its roof structure.

Alveoli in the human lung look like some structures built by ants and humans *(figs. 17.12 and 17.13).*

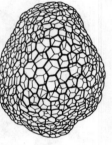

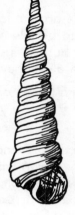

17.6.

17.7.
U.S. Pavilion, Montreal; Buckminster Fuller, 1967.

17.8.

17.9.

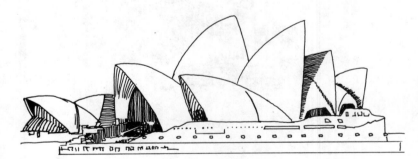

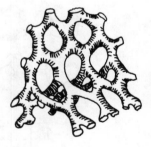

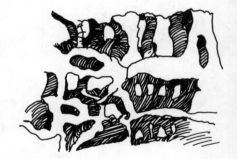

17.10
Sydney Opera House, Australia; Jorn Utzon, 1959-1973.

17.11

17.12.
Lungs.

17.13.
Red ant structure.

This market place in Royan, France *(fig. 17.14)*, by André Morisseau, looks surprisingly like some large white shells found in the ocean *(fig. 17.15)*.

Because **rock** is such an important part of nature, buildings using stone as a construction material often seem more natural or **organic.** *Figure 17.16* is a simple pioneer rock house. Even though it is still basically a box, the stone surface harmonizes with the trees, ivy, and environment.

Figure 17.17 shows some natural forms which could be used for ideas in planning buildings. These are soap bubble cells. Have you ever filled your tub with bubble bath and watched how each bubble is shaped by the pressure of bubbles next to it? While the cells look very much alike, they are all different. No two appear to be the same.

Many forms in nature are based on crystals *(fig. 17.18)*. Even though geometric (regular shape, straight lines), they are very different from one another. *Figure 17.19* is a synagogue in Israel.

Because of convenience, it is a tendency of architectural designers to work with "boxes," that is, with things easily drawn with straight edges, right triangles, T-squares, and compasses *(fig. 17.20)*. As a result, many "natural forms" alternatives are ignored or rejected as too bothersome. For example, it is easy to design the building in *figure 17.21* using straight edges and rulers.

17.14.
Market place, Royan, France; André Morisseau, c. 1950.

17.15.
Shell.

17.16.

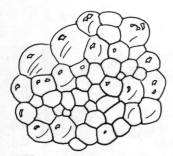

17.17.

17.18.

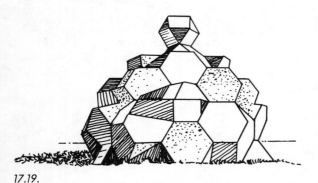

17.19.

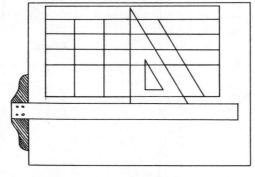

17.20.

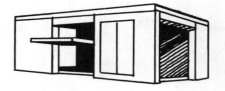

17.21.

But buildings like those in *figure 17.22* require a whole new set of skills, tools, and attitudes. These homes are more natural—softer, less harsh forms. Though similar, they enjoy unlimited variation.

Sometimes the only way we can get our buildings to satisfy our need to be part of **nature** is with **landscape architecture.** We plant flowers, grass, bushes, and trees or ivy to make us feel more welcome, or attracted to the otherwise harsh design.

17.22.
Rural community, Trulli, near Cisternino, Italy.

PRODUCTIVE THINKING

Name 20 things found in nature. What kinds of things are *not* found in nature?

Can you think of some things in nature that give you an idea for a house or a building? What are they?

What are all of the ways a tree house is **natural?** *(Fig. 17.23)* (It is wood, in a tree, kind of haphazardly built, etc.) **Unnatural?**

17.23

SUGGESTED ACTIVITIES

Find some forms in nature—walking home, around your house, on a visit to the mountains or the beach, in biology books—which you think would be interesting ideas for buildings. *(See figs. 17.24 through 17.26.)*

17.24.
Wood

17.25.
Seed pods

17.26.
Shell

Cut snowflakes *(fig. 17.27)*, then use them as special windows in a building you draw, or trace them and make them **dimensional** by adding a few lines.

Find pictures in magazines of buildings which look like they were inspired by natural things.

Fill a milk carton with partially inflated balloons. Then fill the carton with plaster *(figs. 17.28 and 17.29)*. Let it set, then pop the balloons and peel away the carton. A **natural** form will be made. (You can carve and "improve" the form with a knife or a rasp.)

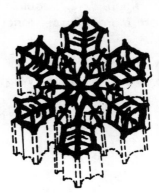

17.27.

17.28.

17.29.

CONCEPT

Scale is the size relationship of two things or parts to the whole.

LESSON

Proportion is a mathematical relationship of things. **Scale** is how we see the **size** relationship of things. We tend to use objects of familiar size as measuring devices to tell us how big a building is. *(See fig. 18.1.)*

There are two basic measuring tools we use. One is based on our experiences with **typical objects,** such as bricks, rocks, doors, or windows *(fig. 18.2).* The other common tool is the human body itself. We then compare these typical objects to the human scale and other objects and buildings.

Everything in a building has a **size.** The size of each element is seen either in comparison to the objects around it, or to our human bodies, as in *figure 18.3.*

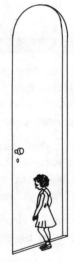

18.1.
The size of the trees alters the scale/size of the building in these two renditions.

18.2.
If we focus in on only one window, with a person silhouetted in it, the scene may be entirely different from a group of windows or compared to a giant window on the same wall.

18.3.

E

Thomas Jefferson designed the rotunda at the University of Virginia *(fig. 18.4)*. He got his idea for it from the architect Palladio and the Pantheon of Ancient Rome *(fig. 18.5)*. It is an interesting building to look at in terms of scale, because the main entry has columns and an entrance pediment. These columns and pediment are in scale with the **exterior** of the building. The wall behind the columns has doors and windows which are scaled to the humans who will use the building, and they are in scale with the **interior** of the building.

According to the ancient Greek mathematicians, a **ratio** refers to a quantitative comparison of like things, but **proportion** refers to the **equality** of those ratios— a constant quality of **relationship** which exists between any ratios.

18.4.
University of Virginia, rotunda, Charlottesville, Virginia; Thomas Jefferson, 1786.

18.5.
The Pantheon, Rome; A.D. **118-125.**

PRODUCTIVE THINKING

Make a list of small things. Compare things on the list to other things which are smaller or larger than those listed. For example, if one thing on the list of small things is "cat," then is the cat small next to a butterfly? Is it small next to an elephant? To tell how big something is requires **comparing** it to something else.

Look at a map of your city. The map does not *really* show how big the city is. But it is to **scale.** This means that a street on the map is as long in comparison to a park as in the real world—it is four times as long as the park, etc. A photograph of you is to scale—so, even though small, it looks just like you.

Architects often make drawings of buildings using ¼ inch to equal one foot. If they want the drawing to be even smaller, they can use ⅛ inch to be one actual foot *(fig. 18.6)*.

We can use anything we want to measure size relationships. How many pencils wide is your desk? (Four? Four and a half? Are all pencils the same size?) Horses are measured by hands. *Figure 18.7* is a horse which is ten hands tall to his withers.

Devise at least ten ways to measure the size of a single object. Which is larger, a brick or a board? A rock or a window?

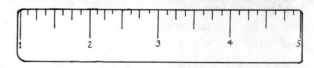

18.6.

18.7.

Figure 18.8 is the famous Empire State Building in New York City. Draw something beside it which is very much out of scale. Draw something else beside it which is *in* scale.

Name things which are about as large as your hand. What are some things which are as big as your house? Draw a door on a wall, and then draw your family to scale, by that door.

Make a map of your city, neighborhood, or yard. The distances should be to **scale.**

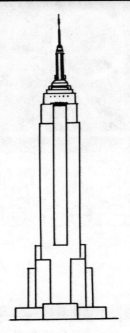

18.8.
Empire State Building, New York; Shreve, Lamb, and Harmon, 1933.

3/19

All views of a building should be considered as it is planned.

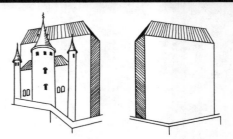

Do we look the same from the front and the back? How about the side? What are all of the ways we recognize our friends, regardless of whether we see them from the front or the back *(figs. 19.1 and 19.2)*? (By clothes we know are theirs; the way they are shaped; how they talk, walk, stand; their size, hair, and proportion—their "essence" or "gestalt.")

All of the views are interesting and helpful. Architects must consider how the building will look from all around it. They try to make every view interesting and beautiful.

19.1.

19.2.

c

City planners should consider various views of important buildings, parks, and scenes so that the city enjoys beautiful vistas or views. Which of these views of the dome of St. Paul's cathedral in London do you enjoy most *(figs. 19.3 and 19.4)*?

The old western United States boom towns (nineteenth century) utilized false front buildings. Designers imagined that people would only see the street front view.

Figures 19.5 through 19.7 show three views of the famous Notre Dame du Haut by Le Corbusier (lay KOR-boos-ee-ay) in Ronchamp, France. He thought about each view as he planned this cathedral. Can you choose a favorite view? The view in *fig. 19.5* is more sculptural. *Figure 19.7* shows a more cubist view.

19.5.
Notre Dame du Haut, France; Le Corbusier, 1950-55.

19.6.

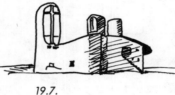

19.7.

19.3.
St. Paul's Cathedral, London; Sir Christopher Wren, 1675-1710.

The traditional view.

19.4.
The "new" view.

What would the object in *figure 19.8* look like from the **top?**

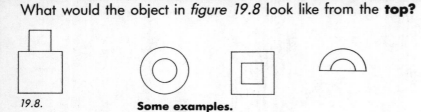

19.8. **Some examples.**

What would *figure 19.9* look like from the **side** view? (This is the **top** view.)

19.9. **Some examples.**

How many more views of the object in *figure 19.10* could you draw?

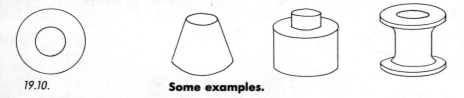

19.10. **Some examples.**

SUGGESTED ACTIVITY

Cognitive/Convergent: (See exercises in productive thinking on drawing various views.)

Divergent: Model an unusual form (not too complex), then draw three unusual views of it.

Imagine viewing a tree in the yard from **above** it in a helicopter. Make drawings of what it would look like. Do this for some playground equipment. Do it for your home. (These are marvelous imagery/visual thinking exercises leading to the ability to read a set of architectural floor plans.)

3/20

Forms and shapes have optical weight influenced by texture and color.

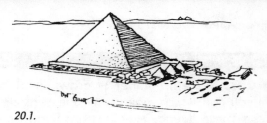

Notice how **heavy** the pyramid *(fig. 20.1)* appears when compared to the domed Hagia Sophia in Istanbul *(fig. 20.2)*. This is because of the feeling that the big pyramid is "settling down" and is **solid.** The Hagia Sophia has a dome which "floats" above the rest of the building. The minarets help it achieve a lighter, more graceful look.

In *figures 20.3 and 20.4,* color the big roof of Corbusier's chapel at Ronchamp, France, in a **light** color, such as light yellow. Now which building appears to be heavier?

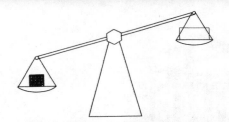

20.1.

20.4.

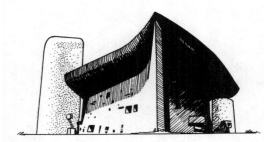

20.3.
Notre Dame du Haut, France; Le Corbusier, 1950-1955.

20.2.
Hagia Sophia, Istanbul, Turkey; A.D. **532-537.**

C

Compare the domed Taj Mahal *(fig. 20.5)* with the domed Roman Pantheon *(fig. 20.6).* Which one **feels** lighter to you? (Most people would say that the Taj Mahal feels lighter in appearance because of the more graceful curves on the dome and its minaret on top. The Pantheon is so geometric and spherical that it rests heavily on the drum supporting it.)

One of the reasons forms feel lighter or heavier is because of our **experience.** We have observed that a **pile** of blocks *(fig. 20.7)* is heavier than a **structure** of blocks *(fig. 20.8),* often simply because more blocks are required to reach the same height.

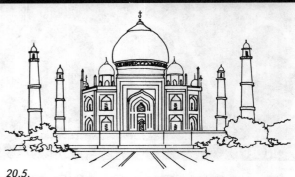

20.5.
Taj Mahal, Agra, India; 1632-1654.

20.6.
The Pantheon, Rome, A.D. 118-125.

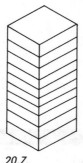

20.7.
A pile (heavier)

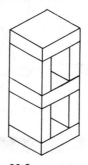

20.8.
A structure (lighter)

PRODUCTIVE THINKING

Warm-ups: Make a number of drawings of **heavy** things, or draw all of the little sketches you can which make someone think **light.** *(See the sketches in figure 20.9 for examples.)* These fluency exercises are important. Be sure to do them.

What are some ways you could make a roof lighter?

Analogies: Heavy is to light as _____ is to _____.

Simile: The wall was as light as _____.

Be sure to use your creativity once you see how "warm-ups" work in divergent thinking, to write your own exercises, analogies, and similes.

SCALE AT ZERO , WEIGHTLESS, "LIGHT",

BY ASSOCIATION, , BALLOON LIFT,

USE LIGHT PARTS, BLOW IT UP , BALSA

20.9.

Cognitive: Identify whether buildings (from photographs) are light or heavy in appearance.

Photocopy or trace a simple building, then use tracing paper to change the building in some way to look either heavier or lighter *(fig. 20.10).* (Common approaches include larger roofs, lightened roofs with parts becoming structural, new colors or textures, blockier or less blocky looks, etc.)

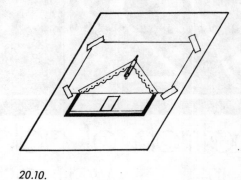

20.10.

4/21

Repetition of color, line, shape, texture, or values can create the feeling of rhythm, pattern, or movement in architectural design.

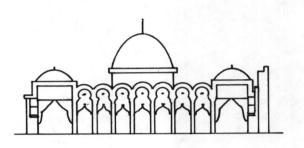

This lesson will seem very elementary, until the sequence pattern is analyzed.

Start with a clapping exercise. This will allow you to feel the rhythm of repetition and also give a starting place for discussing the nature of **repeating** something in various sequences or patterns.

Begin with four steady beats per measure. Clap: 1-2-3-4/1-2-3-4/1-2-3-4, etc. For variety, keep the steady beat with other movements as well (four each: slap thighs, tap toes, snap fingers, tap top of head, clap hands, click tongue, move head from side to side, etc.). More variety can be created by doubling some beats. Clap the name of your town and those near you. One-syllable names get one beat, two-syllable names get two claps per beat.

21.1.

Salt Lake City, Utah

B

Any clapping exercises may be tied into a music experience as well. It is logical to **transfer** from clapping a rhythm to another art form. Dance is a logical choice. The rhythm of a painting, sculpture, or piece of architecture is usually not noticed as easily as in music or dance. Architects often plan the repetition in their buildings to establish motion (movement) just as musicians and dancers do. Repetition usually has a **unifying** effect in a design.

One of the things which makes rhythm so interesting is its **relation to time.** One does not fully understand the concept of rhythm until it is seen in a runner *(fig. 21.2),* ice skater, building, or painting, or until heard in music or sensed in nature—as in the rising and setting sun, wind and trees, heart beats, or the seasons. All of these occur in a **time** setting (the sun in 24-hour periods, the heart beat per minute, and the runner according to distance and velocity).

Visual rhythm is perhaps the most beautiful of all rhythms when fully perceived. Its most simple expression is linear. This is a simple "lining up" of colors, shapes, values, or textures. These elements may be lined up by size, shape, or detail in variations. For example, with a repeated **shape,** varied in **size,** we get the linear rhythm shown in *figure 21.3.*

Now, by including detail variations with *un*like shapes, we would get the linear rhythm found in *figure 21.4.* We would call this a "triangular rhythm motif" because the unifying thread is triangular repetition.

Why is *figure 21.5* called a rhythmic line? It is because the waves **repeat,** just like clapping a sequence. In fact, surfers know that waves come in sequence, and this helps them to know when the *big* wave will be coming. By counting, they know that the fourth wave will be large—and tomorrow it may be every fifth wave.

Like balance, rhythm may be radial—where repetition may go spinning in a block or a spiral *(see figs. 21.6-21.8).*

Figure 21.9 is Frank Lloyd Wright's Marin County Courthouse in California. How has he created rhythm by repetition? (Repeated circular windows, wave-like curves, details on cornice.)

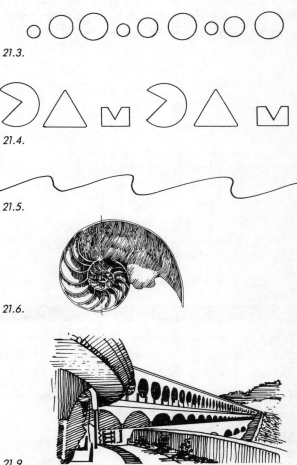

21.2.

21.3.

21.4.

21.5.

21.6.

21.7.
Thanksgiving Square Chapel, Dallas; Philip Johnson and John Burgee, 1977.

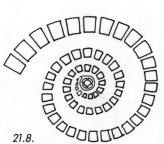

21.8.

21.9.
Marin County Courthouse, Santa Venitia, California; Frank Lloyd Wright, 1957, remodeled 1970.

It is important to realize that the human eye tends to give its attention in specific ways. For example, it loves to follow along an edge; it always seeks out detail *(figs. 21.10 and 21.11)*.

The eye will give attention to **contrast,** whether color, line, texture, shape, or value *(fig. 21.12)*.

The eye will follow **repetition** *(fig. 21.13)*.

This tendency of the eye to "follow along" and give attention to particular effects is what gives the feeling of movement to visual rhythm. Such repetitive, rhythmic qualities often enhance the **unity** in a design. They help us see **order** in the composition.

In the ancient temple in Greece *(fig. 21.14)*, the columns repeat and set up a rhythm, but so do the dark spaces between the columns. This **alternating rhythm** invites our eyes to follow along the columns.

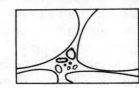
21.10.

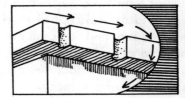
21.11.

21.12.

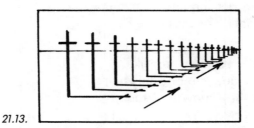
21.13.

21.14.
Temple of Hepthaistos, Athens, Greece; c. 449 B.C.

What are some repetitive visual experiences you may see on a walk through town? (Parked autos, moving autos, fence posts, chain link fences, clouds, leaves, sidewalk sections, parking meters, flowers, rocks, other people, trees, etc. The list is endless.)

If you took a walk in nature (mountains, beach, woods), what ways would you see that nature has repeated things?

Simile: Music without rhythm is like _____. (Racing without running, dancing without moving.)

Analogy: Wall surface is to detail or decoration as _____ is to _____. (Music, rhythm.) You think up a better analogy.

Cognitive: Draw a 3" x 6" wall *(fig. 21.15)*. Decorate this wall surface by repeating something to create rhythm *(see fig. 21.16)*.

Divergent: Design a space station which has interesting repetitive rhythmic qualities in its windows, doors, roof, equipment, and so on *(see fig. 21.17)*.

Perception of rhythmic repetition depends on ability to see likeness. Exercises like the ones which follow help sharpen such perception.

Which one differs? Try the puzzles in *figures 21.18-21.20*. These exercises help to develop recognition of subtle differences while still keeping with a rigid, basic rhythmic essence. (The highest skill for a person to discover in exercises like these is to find the solution by "feel," rather than careful analysis. "Feel" is right-brained.)

Figure 21.21 shows that a general or essential flow of rhythm can occur when the elements are quite different, yet maintain a basic similarity.

A walk to look for visual rhythm in the neighborhood would be a useful activity.

21.15.

21.16.

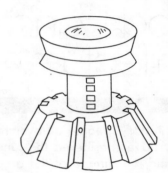

21.17.

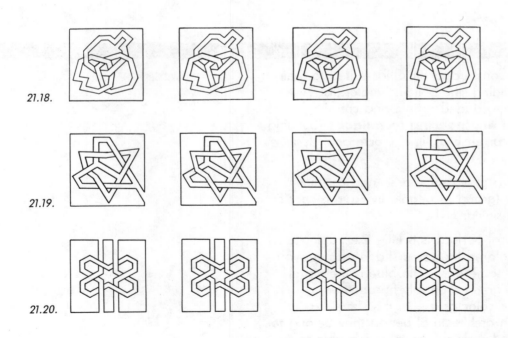

21.18.

21.19.

21.20.

21.21.
Rural community, Trulli, near Cisternino, Italy.

LEVEL / ACTIVITY

4/22A

CONCEPT

There are specific visual clues to identifying styles, themes, periods, and movements in architecture.

LESSON

Throughout history, people all over the world have constructed buildings suited to their needs. They have considered the function of the building, the building materials available, and the climate of the area. They have also added artistic and creative touches based on an ever-growing understanding of **engineering techniques** (building methods). Style is determined as a coincidental concurrence of time, place, and idea or philosophy.

There have been **periods** when all the buildings in a geographic area had certain **common** characteristics. Within each main **culture** (group of people living in a specific geographic area), the buildings were designed in a similar style.

Recognizing *which* buildings fit into *which* architectural periods is a little like putting a jigsaw puzzle together. If you have several pieces colored the same shade of blue, you can be pretty sure that they all fit into basically the same area. The blue is the visual clue you need. All the pieces with similar shades of green probably fit together somehow, based on the visual clue you get from the color green. In the same way, structures and buildings give visual clues as to which architectural period they belong to. We can learn a lot about a people, their history, and their culture by being able to recognize and identify these architectural clues.

B

Architectural history is broken down into several major periods or eras in this book:

I.   Prehistoric Era

II.   The Ancient World Period

III.   Early Christian Period

IV.   Medieval Period (including Romanesque and Gothic)

V.   Renaissance Period

VI.   Baroque Period (including Mannerism and Rococo)

VII. Revolutionary Period (Neoclassic, Romantic)

VIII. Twentieth Century Styles

We are going to look at a few examples from each of these periods and learn some **visual** clues for each. Then you can begin to identify where various buildings fit into the architectural ''puzzle.'' Each major period or era may contain several important and more specific styles or periods within itself. You will enjoy visualizing this historical recognition section, and finding examples in your own community and in your travels.

4/22B

The first general period is called the Ancient World.

One aspect of **visual literacy** relative to cultures is being able to identify the age, place, and style of a structure. In lessons 22B-H, will be given some examples of **visual clues** useful in identifying and categorizing our interesting **built environment.** Many buildings in your city or those nearby are borrowed from others in history.

One approach to this goal is to begin in early history. We can go clear back to prehistory—before there was much in the way of written records. Most of the art and architecture from prehistory has withered away at the hands of earthquakes, winds, rains, floods, temperature changes, and even wars.

We will use a simplified chart of each style and period in history with visual clues to recognize structures from each.

Some of the most significant remnants from prehistoric architecture are the burial mounds, caves, and temples such as Stonehenge in England. We will start there. (It must be mentioned that accurate dating here is next to impossible because carbon 14 dating makes an unverifiable assumption that the chemistry of the atmosphere has remained **constant.** The probability that it *has* been constant is not very high.)

PERIOD OR STYLE	APPROXIMATE DATE	HOW TO RECOGNIZE IT (VISUAL CLUES)	DESCRIPTION
Prehistory	Prehistoric (Paleolithic, Mesolithic, Neolithic)	 *22b.1.* **Stonehenge, Wiltshire, England; prehistory.**	*22b.1.* Building parts not precise; crude; in a state of decay. Served very basic functions, such as for ancient magical religious rites. Very ancient, crude artifacts.
	Prehistoric	 *22b.2.* **Mounds, Central-Eastern U.S.A.; prehistory.**	*22b.2.* Mounds obviously not made by nature—located in an area with no hills and lined up in order and height. Artifacts and human remains buried under the mounds.
Egyptian	4000-332 B.C.	 *22b.3.* **Step Pyramid of Zoser, Saqqara, Egypt; 2750** B.C. *22b.4.* **Pyramid of Khufu, Gizeh, Egypt; 2650** B.C.	*22b.3 and 23b.4.* Masonry construction (stone); (Zoser is oldest masonry structure of its size in existence). Pyramids built in steps, then filled in to make "perfect pyramid" in later dynasties. Related to temples and ancient burial mounds. Enormous scale.

PERIOD OR STYLE	APPROXIMATE DATE	HOW TO RECOGNIZE IT (VISUAL CLUES)	DESCRIPTION
Egyptian (cont'd.)	1257 B.C.	 22b.5. **Rock-cut Tomb of Rameses II, Abu Simbel, Egypt; 1257** B.C.	*22b.5.* Rock-cut; carved rather than built up. Tomb and temple carved as a cave and decorated with sculpture. Sculpture is abstract rather than real or representational.
	1300 B.C.	 22b.6. **Temple of Amen-Re, Karnak, Egypt; c. 1300** B.C.	*22b.6.* Colossal scale. Hypostyle hall—a post and beam system of stone (wood very scarce). Columns like buds or bell-shaped plant forms; decorated shafts.
Mesopotamian/- Neo-Sumerian (Ur)	2100 B.C.	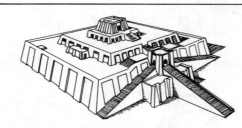 22b.7. **Ziggurat at Ur, Iraq; 2100** B.C.	*22b.7.* Ziggurat form: massive, step pyramid shapes, with giant ramp stairway access. Temples on top.

PERIOD OR STYLE	APPROXIMATE DATE	HOW TO RECOGNIZE IT (VISUAL CLUES)	DESCRIPTION
Greek (Classical or Hellenic)	432 B.C.	 *22b.8.* **The Parthenon, Athens, Greece; Callicrates and Ictinus, 432 B.C.**	*22b.8.* Stone construction: Doric columns; studied proportions (golden mean). Low gable is called pediment. Stylobate curved to appear flat or horizontal. Columns curved to appear parallel.
	421 B.C.	 *22b.9.* **Erechtheum, Acropolis, Athens, Greece; 421-405 B.C.**	*22b.9.* Sculpture (statuary) on buildings; relief sculpture illustration on frieze and pediment. Caryatids (maiden columns) on Erechtheum at Athens. Women as sculpted columns.
	530 B.C.	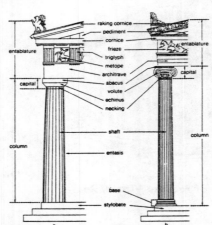 *22b.10.*	*22b.10.* The Doric, Ionic, and Corinthian orders.

Labels in figure 22b.10: raking cornice, pediment, cornice, entablature, frieze, triglyph, metope, architrave, abacus, capital, volute, echinus, necking, entablature, capital, shaft, column, column, entasis, base, stylobate

PERIOD OR STYLE	APPROXIMATE DATE	HOW TO RECOGNIZE IT (VISUAL CLUES)	DESCRIPTION
Greek (Hellenistic, later period)	175 B.C.	 *22b.11.* **Altar of Zeus and Athena, Pergamum, Greece; c. 175** B.C.	*22b.11.* Sculpted reliefs now on "first floor" (pedestal) rather than the pediments or friezes. Less idealized proportions and sculpture; more realistic, expressive, and emotional. Higher stylobates.
Roman (Early and Etruscan)	450 B.C.	 *22b.12.* **Necropolis at Caere, Italy; c. 450** B.C.	*22b.12.* Hemispherical roofs of stone. Partly underground.
	190 B.C.	 *22b.13.* **Classical Temple of Fortuna Virnes, Rome, Italy; c. 190** B.C.	*22b.13.* Classical Greek influence from Ionic order. Stylobate is now only a stairway up a platform. Some columns "attached."

PERIOD OR STYLE	APPROXIMATE DATE	HOW TO RECOGNIZE IT (VISUAL CLUES)	DESCRIPTION
Roman (cont'd.)	50 B.C. to A.D. 285	 *22b.14.* **Ancient Roman apartments called ''insula.''**	*22b.14.* Hipped roof. Three to five stories. Brick and concrete. Ground floor walls larger, with shops, etc. (Later to influence Renaissance palazzo style.) Most are in ruins.
	50 B.C.	 *22b.15.* **Roman arch in aqueducts.**	*22b.15.* The arcade principle to span large distances. The arch as Rome's creative contribution.
	A.D. 120	 *22b.16.* **The Pantheon, Rome, Italy; A.D. 118-125.**  *22b.17.* **The Pantheon, Rome, Italy; interior.**	*22b.16 and 22b.17.* Arch now used as a dome (hemispherical). Classical pediment and columns as facade. Significant (large) interior spaces. Oculus or ''eye'' in dome left open.

PERIOD OR STYLE	APPROXIMATE DATE	HOW TO RECOGNIZE IT (VISUAL CLUES)	DESCRIPTION
Roman (cont'd)	A.D. 70		*22b.18.* Oval plan, arcade structure. Recreational function.

22b.18. **Colosseum Amphitheater, Rome, Italy; A.D. 70.**

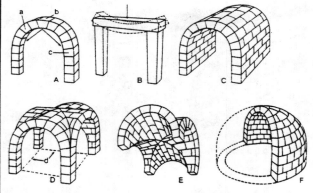

22b.19. **Roman use of arch in structural innovation.**

22b.19.

A — shows keystone (b) thrust points (c) and voussoirs (a).

B — shows beam in deflection—compressed on top, stretched on bottom.

C — shows extended or "thick" arch to make a vault.

D & E — shows vaults intersecting to form a groin vault.

F — a rotated arch makes a dome.

22b.20. **Roman Triumphal Arch.**

PERIOD OR STYLE	APPROXIMATE DATE	HOW TO RECOGNIZE IT (VISUAL CLUES)	DESCRIPTION
Roman (cont'd)	A.D. 81		22b.21. Corinthian order.
	A.D. 80		22b.22 Tall middle section with side aisles has shed roof; (an influence on Christian cathedrals).

22b.22. **Basilica idea.**

4/22C

The second general period is called Early Christian.

Following the persecution of Christians, the Roman emperor Constantine saw a political opportunity to unite a split kingdom by declaring Christianity the official Roman religion in 325 A.D. With this Age of Recognition, a whole new architectural spirit took root. Within five years, the Christians erected Old St. Peter's Cathedral (now torn down, but drawings such as the above logo still exist). For their style they combined the old Roman basilican form, ideas from their catacomb chapels, and features from atrium houses of ancient Rome.

The chart for the Early Christian Period begins with the basilica structure borrowed from Ancient Rome. The Christians divided themselves into Eastern and Western styles, centering in Constantinople and Rome, respectively.

PERIOD OR STYLE	APPROXIMATE DATE	HOW TO RECOGNIZE IT (VISUAL CLUES)	DESCRIPTION
Early Christian, Western	A.D. 330-800 (and on into later periods)	*22c.1.* *22c.2.*	*22c.1 and 22c.2.* The basilica style with large center space and smaller lower side aisles. Floor plan in form of a cross.
Early Christian, Western (cont'd.)	A.D. 533	*22c.3.* **Sant' Apollinare in Classe, Ravenna, Italy; c. A.D. 533-549.**	*22c.3.* Other forms cluster about the center, dominating form. Floor plan is rectangular. Bell tower (campanile) and baptistry part of the compound. Exterior is austere (plain).
Early Christian, Eastern	A.D. 533	*22c.5.* *22c.4.* **San Vitale, Ravenna, Italy; A.D. 526-547.**	*22c.4 and 22c.5.* Eastern plans were radially balanced or central. Other forms cluster about the center, dominating form. Both Christian styles turned the old classical Greek temple "outside in," that is, the columns and decoration are within, while the flat walls are on the exterior.

PERIOD OR STYLE	APPROXIMATE DATE	HOW TO RECOGNIZE IT (VISUAL CLUES)	DESCRIPTION
Early Christian, Eastern (cont'd.)	A.D. 532	 *22c.6.*　**Hagia Sophia, Istanbul, Turkey;** A.D. **532-537.**	*22c.6.* Minor forms cluster about the major form— the dome. The plan is "Eastern." Now an Islamic mosque.
Islamic	A.D. 848	 *22c.7.*　**Great Mosque of Samarra, Iraq;** A.D. 848-852  *22c.8.*　**Great Mosque of Samarra, plan.**	*22c.7.* Minaret: spiral tower. *22c.8. and 22c.9.* Plan shows "forest" of columns to hold up flat and multi-domed roof, which is now in ruin on the ground.

PERIOD OR STYLE	APPROXIMATE DATE	HOW TO RECOGNIZE IT (VISUAL CLUES)	DESCRIPTION
Islamic (cont'd.)		 *22c.9.* **Great Mosque of Samarra, interior.**	
	A.D. 1632	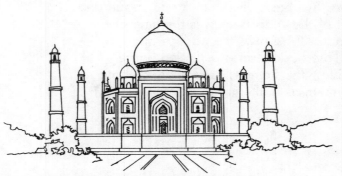 *22c.10.* **Taj Mahal, Agra, India; 1632-1654.**	*22c.10.* Central plan and dome. Minarets at yard corners. Abstract design patterns as opposed to pictures of humans and animals.

4/22D

CONCEPT

The third general period is called Medieval.

LESSON

Once the early Christians became the "establishment," the Western Christian styles matured into the Medieval Period. This period has two basic divisions—Romanesque and Gothic. The Romanesque Period, where this part of the chart begins, is the time of knights and ladies, monks, castles, and the crusades. It borrows the basilica and rounded arch forms from ancient Roman styles. (The basic form is a gabled, large central structure with shed roofs covering side aisles. The Romans used them for bath houses and palaces, while Early Christians used them as gathering places to worship.)

PERIOD OR STYLE	APPROXIMATE DATE	HOW TO RECOGNIZE IT (VISUAL CLUES)	DESCRIPTION
Romanesque	1001	 *22d.1.* **Abbey Church of St. Michael, Hildesheim, Germany; c. 1001-1030.**	*22d.1.* Blocky geometric look—rectangles, cubes, cones, and cylinders grouped together. Rectangular (Western plan). Round arch windows; (main floor "pointed" windows were added during Gothic Period).
	1080	 *22d.2.* **The nave of St. Sernin, Toulouse, France; 1080-1120.**	*22d.2.* Exterior structure is expressed more than in early Christian styles (buttressing, roof supports, etc.). Interior expresses a round arched barrel vault, similar to those in Ancient Rome, but higher and more vertical. Interior is still simple. Exterior now more elaborate than Early Christian style. Height and mass is greater. Round arch windows and entries.
	1053-1272	 *22d.3.* **Pisa Cathedral, Pisa, Italy; 1053-1272.**	*22d.3.* The famous "Leaning Tower of Pisa" is the bell tower (campanile) of Pisa Cathedral, a Romanesque structure which is a nearly ideal expression of the old basilica form, now made more vertical. Round arch windows, broad transept, separate baptistry, tower, and cathedral.

PERIOD OR STYLE	APPROXIMATE DATE	HOW TO RECOGNIZE IT (VISUAL CLUES)	DESCRIPTION
Romanesque (cont'd.)		 *22d.4.* **Tower of London, England; 1081.**	*22d.4.* Castlelike battlements. Fortress look. Round arch entries and windows.
Gothic	1248	 *22d.5.* **Notre Dame Cathedral, Paris; 1163-1250.**	*22d.5.* Two entry towers at east entry; entry has three doors. Exterior very detailed and decorated; (remember how simply Romanesque wall surfaces were articulated?). Rose window (round). Pointed arch window. Stained glass. Flying buttresses.

PERIOD OR STYLE	APPROXIMATE DATE	HOW TO RECOGNIZE IT (VISUAL CLUES)	DESCRIPTION
Gothic (cont'd.)	1163-1250 1248	 *22d.6.* **Notre Dame Cathedral, Paris; 1163-1250.** 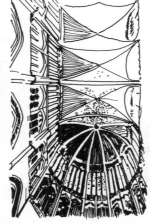 *22d.7.* **Amiens Cathedral, Amien, France; 1220-1236.** *22d.8.* **Choir vault of Amiens Cathedral.** 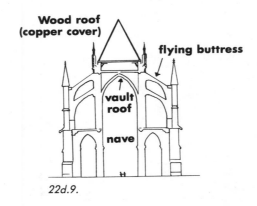 *22d.9.*	*22d.6.* Exteriors carved and elaborated with sculpture. Notre Dame is an ideal Gothic structure. Flying buttresses. Much stained glass. Rose windows. Double entry towers. Central spire. Gargoyles (grotesque figures to frighten away evil spirits and serve as drains from the roof). *22d.7 and 22d.8.* Interiors now use pointed arch vaults which intersect (groin vaults). Columns carved in detail, like a group of trees spreading into a ceiling. Ceiling "floats" upon clerestory. (The Romanesque Period used very little in window openings.) High, vertical feeling. *22d.9.* Tiny people show scale of the enormous nave vault in the basilican structure.

Labels in figure 22d.9.: Wood roof (copper cover), flying buttress, vault roof, nave

PERIOD OR STYLE	APPROXIMATE DATE	HOW TO RECOGNIZE IT (VISUAL CLUES)	DESCRIPTION
Gothic (cont'd.)	1386	 22d.10. **Milan Cathedral, Italy; 1386.**	*22d.10 and 22d.11.* The Gothic is pushed to a point of virtually no more wall surface left to carve, sculpt, or decorate. Compare this highly articulated wall treatment to the old Romanesque Cathedral of Saint Ambrogio in Milan, Italy.
	1120	 22d.11. **Saint Ambrogio, Milan, Italy; c. 1090-1120.**	

The fourth general period is called the Renaissance.

The Gothic cathedral, as seen in Milan, Italy, became so detailed and so open to stained glass expression that there was no further elaboration possible. Architects were ready to look for a new approach. Because of renewed discovery of the Ancient Roman and Greek cultures by archaeologists, the classical influence became the "new." This rediscovery of classical order, geometry, and proportion was expressed in their new buildings. The Renaissance had begun. The city of Florence, Italy, was the center of this new era. The old cathedral had a hole for a dome, but no one could design such a large one. Finally, Brunelleschi solved the problem, and a Renaissance dome was built using Gothic technology.

PERIOD OR STYLE	APPROXIMATE DATE	HOW TO RECOGNIZE IT (VISUAL CLUES)	DESCRIPTION
The Renaissance	1420	22e.1. **Florence Cathedral, Italy; Brunelleschi, 1420-1436.**	*22e.1.* The old cathedral has a Romanesque campanile, a Gothic nave, but large, lanterned dome. The Gothic look is concealed. The dome is at the center of the birth of the Renaissance—a transitional building. The graceful domes of the Baroque Period will grow out of these early domes.
	1440	22e.2. **Pazzi Chapel, Florence, Italy; Brunelleschi, c.1400. (Early forerunner to Renaissance.)**	*22e.2.* A radial pediment over doorway; central dome. Modular spaces built to mathematical ratios. Classical Roman columns which are attached pilasters on main floor and second. Remind yourself how different this approach is in light of the Gothic style, which it follows in time. Renaissance architects used the new form of the ribbed dome to show dominance over a unified cluster of other forms.
	1502	22e.3. **Tempietto S. Pietro, Rome; Donate Bramante, 1502.**	*22e.3.* The pilasters on the drum repeat the feeling of going upward and lead the eye past the cornice to the ribs of the dome.

PERIOD OR STYLE	APPROXIMATE DATE	HOW TO RECOGNIZE IT (VISUAL CLUES)	DESCRIPTION
The Renaissance	1502	 **22e.4.** **Temple of Sibyl, Tivoli, Italy; early 1st century** A.D.	*22e.4.* The new classical feeling is similar to small pagan Roman temples like the Temple of Sibyl in Tivoli.
		 **22e.5.** **Santa Maria Della Consolazione, Todi, Italy; Donato Bramante, 1502.**	*22e.5.* The banister (balustrade) has a rhythm like the colonnade, but shorter ''beats,'' and it controls a too-abrupt ascent to the dome. A substantial lantern controls upward thrusts. Notice the lantern on top of the dome of Santa Maria Dell Consolazione. It is no longer only ''sculptural,'' but is a tiny room.
	1535	 **22e.6.** **Ancient Roman apartments.**	*22e.6.* Usually three stories, occasionally four. Large roof cornice. Main floor more Romanesque or fortress-looking. Pediments over the windows. Often uses classical orders in columns of windows—Corinthian on top floor, Ionic on second floor, Doric or Tuscan on main floor, if at all.

PERIOD OR STYLE	APPROXIMATE DATE	HOW TO RECOGNIZE IT (VISUAL CLUES)
The Renaissance	1547	

22e.7. **Michelangelo's Dome of St. Peter's Cathedral, Rome; dome completed c. 1590, facade by Carlo Maderna.**

22e.7. The columns of the drum of the dome are doubled Corinthian. (The Baroque architects will re-use this idea again and again.)

The lantern is now highly ornate.

As the High or Late Renaissance arrived, men such as Michelangelo and Bramante carried the dome of Rome and Eastern Early Christians to new beauty in form, proportion, and surface treatment.

22e.8. Many buildings will use St. Peter's as a model, including St. Paul's in London, the U.S. Capitol in Washington, D.C., and the state capitol buildings in Utah, California, Colorado, and many others.

The Cathedral of St. Peter's Basilica would lead into new periods—the Mannerist and then the Baroque.

22e.8. **Villa Rotunda, Vicenza, Italy; Palladio, c. 1550-1553.**

Of interest: the facade by Maderna violated certain orders of proportion which Michelangelo and Bramante had originally planned. First, they had anticipated a central plan, but Maderna extended the nave in the Western fashion, the effect of which "shrunk" the dome. As one approaches, the drum is barely visible now. Second, the rhythm of the columns starts wide at sides and gets closer to the pediment in an awkward rhythm. The pediment itself is too small for the rest of the facade.

4/22F

The fifth general period is called the Baroque. (The Baroque began with Mannerism and ended with the Rococo style.)

The great Renaissance architects were also great sculptors, painters, poets, inventors, scientists, and philosophers. They were so great that some young architects and artists became self-conscious and were intimidated by the great works of the Renaissance masters. As a result of this lack of confidence to go beyond such greatness, they became satisfied to "copy"—to work **in the manner of** Da Vinci, Raphael, Bramante, and Michelangelo. Because of this they were called "Mannerists." Other Mannerists were confidently **breaking** with the Renaissance classical rules of design.

The Mannerists took one of two possible directions: (1) They could do exacting copies of the old masters and classic models. (2) They could make fun of the problem and rebel, breaking the Renaissance rules of order and proportion. Many chose this second option as their "manner" of working. They loved to shock people with their departures from classical order. One of those to play with classical rules was Romano. Another important Mannerist architect was Palladio. Almost every community in the world has a building which copies one by Palladio (fig. 22f.1).

22f.1.
Villa Rotunda, Vicenza, Italy; Palladio, c. 1550-1553.

PERIOD OR STYLE	APPROXIMATE DATE	HOW TO RECOGNIZE IT (VISUAL CLUES)	DESCRIPTION
Baroque-Mannerism	1525	 22f.2. **Romano's court facade at Palazzo Del Te, Mantua, Italy; 1525-1535.**	*22f.2.* Romano's joke is to shock those who know classical design. These are the "broken" rules: 1. Windows in frieze and off-center. 2. The architrave lets midstones "slip" down. It is too thin. 3. The stones in "fake windows" have slipped down.
	1566	 22f.3. **S. Giorgio Maggiore, Venice; Andrea Palladio, 1566-1610.**	*22f.3.* Palladio designed this beautiful church in Venice, Italy, to unify the tall central nave and side aisles. He put a classical front porch upon the nave, but made it project out of a lower classical porch by breaking the pediment over the side aisles and first floor. This is a Mannerist approach to using classical form.

PERIOD OR STYLE	APPROXIMATE DATE	HOW TO RECOGNIZE IT (VISUAL CLUES)	DESCRIPTION
Baroque	1590-1750	 *22f.4.* **Santa Susanna, Rome; Carlo Maderna, 1597-1603.**	*22f.4.* Classical pediment and facade synthesize existing motifs. Double (paired) pilasters similar to Michelangelo's on St. Peter's drum. Scroll buttresses. First and second story are well unified with a horizontal rhythm of pilasters and columns climaxing at the central bay.
	1631	 *22f.5.* **Santa Maria del salute, Venice; Longhena, 1631-1682.**	*22f.5.* A break with the stiff, rectilinear style of the Renaissance and Mannerists. Octagonal plan, central. Roman Triumphal Arch entry with pediment. Main entry "echoed" by the other seven sides. Ornamental scroll buttresses. The "whole" remains unified even though the surfaces are highly elaborate.

PERIOD OR STYLE	APPROXIMATE DATE	HOW TO RECOGNIZE IT (VISUAL CLUES)	DESCRIPTION
Baroque (cont'd.)	1665	 *22f.6.* **San Carlo alle Quattro Fontane, Rome; Francesco Borromini, 1665-1667.**	*22f.6.* Scalloped cornices. Fountains on corners. Walls curved to soften the geometry. Highly articulated wall surfaces.
	1670	 *22f.7.* **The Louvre, Paris; Perrault, Le Vau, Le Brun, 1667-1670.**	*22f.7.* Paired columns. Spacious and classical. Balustrades on roof as well as first floor line.

PERIOD OR STYLE	APPROXIMATE DATE	HOW TO RECOGNIZE IT (VISUAL CLUES)	DESCRIPTION
Baroque (cont'd.)	1675	 *22f.8.* **St. Paul's Cathedral, London; Sir Christopher Wren, 1675-1710.**	*22f.8.* Scalloped cornices on towers. Towers are in a vertical, stylized classical form. Double columns (pairs) on facade, two levels. Classical pediment for nave. Ribbed dome with highly ornamented lantern. Dome drum better visualized than at St. Peter's. Pediments over windows. Striking unity of style.
Baroque-Rococo	1724	 *22f.9.* **Palace Belvedere, Vienna, Austria; Hildebrandt, 1724.**	*22f.9.* Baroque, but extremely articulated wall surfaces with curvaceous lines and carved relief like ''icing.'' Much sculpture adorns the structure. Rococo decoration used more ''natural'' forms than Baroque, such as sea shells and fruit. It is a ''cult'' of charm, elegance, and beauty.

PERIOD OR STYLE	APPROXIMATE DATE	HOW TO RECOGNIZE IT (VISUAL CLUES)	DESCRIPTION
Baroque-Rococo (cont'd.)	1737	 22f.10. **Salon de la Princesse, Hotel de Soudise, Paris; interior Germaine Boffrand, 1737-1740.**	*22f.10.* The Baroque-Rococo interiors are as much visual clues as the exteriors. The trend was toward more and more ornamentation until, in the Rococo Period, it is described as "cookie icing"—gold leafed with shells, vines, grapes, and fruit. The Baroque interiors generally featured beautiful painted murals. This over-decoration led to the later phrase, "Less is more, and more is less." (Each period in history goes through a stage of high elaboration.)

4/22G

CONCEPT

The sixth general period is called Revolutionary. It begins with the Neoclassic Era and moves to the Romantic Era.

LESSON

As the aristocracy—kings, queens, and privileged few— enjoyed a life of ease, the general population was tired of the injustice of their difficult lives. The American Revolution against King George led the way, and the French Revolution soon followed. The people wanted independently to control their own destinies. The idealists who sought life, liberty, the pursuit of happiness, equality, and fraternity also found the world turned to limited monarchies, democratic republics, fascist and communist states, as well as military dictatorships. The revolt in art and architecture was against the frivolous Rococo styles. The revolutionists wanted ''greatness''—and Ancient Rome met their image. They replaced monarchs such as the French Louis with a republic. They replaced Christianity with a tolerant paganism, and at one time, the Cathedral of Notre Dame was rededicated to the ''goodness of reason.'' Heroism, self-sacrifice, Spartan simplicity, and ''power of the people'' through reason were the new standards. Frivolous, light, elegant, or extravagant art was to be rejected. The result? The Neoclassic Period.

The Romantic idea is one of nostalgic appreciation and empathy for all other ideas. The Neoclassic period is just a romantic notion of the greatness of Greece and Rome. Now the Orient, Middle East, and other past periods are rediscovered. The result is what we call ''eclectic'' architecture. It borrows anything and everything to suit one's preferences.

The Americans and the French sought the no-nonsense forms of antiquity. Our chart begins with Paris as ''the new Rome,'' with the famed Arch of Triumph as our logo.

PERIOD OR STYLE	APPROXIMATE DATE	HOW TO RECOGNIZE IT (VISUAL CLUES)	DESCRIPTION
Neoclassic	1762	 22g.1. **La Madeleine, Paris; Vignon, 1762.**	*22g.1.* Roman temple: steep pediment, pedestal stylobate, Corinthian order. Napoleon's ''temple of glory.''
	1806	 22g.2. **Arch de Triomphe-du Carrousel, Paris; Napoleonic, 1806.**	*22g.2.* A copy of the Roman triumphal arches. Attached Corinthian columns. Barrel vault arches.
	1785	 22g.3. **University of Virginia, rotunda, Charlottesville; Thomas Jefferson, 1785.**	*22g.3.* Copy of Roman Pantheon after Palladio. (By 1814, Napoleon was stopped. The new Rome had collapsed in Paris.)

PERIOD OR STYLE	APPROXIMATE DATE	HOW TO RECOGNIZE IT (VISUAL CLUES)	DESCRIPTION
Romantic (revivals)			**The romantic idea is one of nostalgic appreciation and empathy for all other ideas. The Neoclassic Period is just a romantic notion of the greatness of Greece and Rome. Now the Orient, Middle East, and other past periods are rediscovered. The result is what we call "eclectic" architecture. It borrows anything and everything to suite its needs.** **The Gothic Period was the first to be revived, due to the popularity of Gothic novels in England. The result—a Gothic Revival in architecture as well.**
Gothic Revival	1796 1846 1850	 *22g.4.* **Fonthill Abbey (destroyed), Wiltshire, England; 1796.** *22g.5.* **St. Clotilde, Paris; 1846.** *22g.6.* **Houses of Parliament, London; Barry and Pugin, 1850.**	*22g.4 and 22g.5.* Gothic pointed arch for windows and entry. Gothic central tower. Romanesque battlements along top of walls. Copied Gothic cathedral. *22g.6.* Gothic windows and walls. Gothic towers.

PERIOD OR STYLE	APPROXIMATE DATE	HOW TO RECOGNIZE IT (VISUAL CLUES)	DESCRIPTION
Romantic (cont'd.) Muslim Revival	1821	 22g.7. **Royal Pavilion, Brighton, England; John Nash, 1821.**	*22g.7. and 22g.8.* Minarets on corners. Onion domes. Decoration in abstract geometric shapes. Arcades with Byzantine décor.
	1893	 22g.8. **Saltair Pavilion, Great Salt Lake, Utah; Richard Kletting, 1893.**	
Renaissance Revival	1850	 22g.9. **Library of Ste. Genevieve, Paris; Henri Labrouste, 1850.**	*22g.9.* Main floor "garlands" above the windows. Large cornice. Attached columns (pilasters) of window arcade, top floor. "Romanesque feel" even though Renaissance Revival.

PERIOD OR STYLE	APPROXIMATE DATE	HOW TO RECOGNIZE IT (VISUAL CLUES)	DESCRIPTION
Romantic (cont'd.) Baroque Revival	1861	 22g.10. **Paris Opera House, Paris; Charles Garnier, 1861.**	*22g.10.* Double columns as in The Louvre. Oval pediments. Highly articulated wall surface. Sculpture as part of design.

4/22H

The seventh general period is called Twentieth Century.

At the turn into the twentieth century, architecture found itself facing a realm of marvelously fresh technology and new visions of abstract design, but clutching the Romantic revivals of nostalgic forms from the past. This unusual dilemma leads us into our contemporary world, today. Architects, such as Frank Lloyd Wright, Walter Gropius, Le Corbusier, and Mies van der Rohe, pointed to the absurdity of people catching trains in "Roman baths," working in Renaissance offices, and going to Gothic churches. They felt it was time to be true to their own time, and that buildings should simply fulfill the needs for which they were designed.

The Twentieth Century style was unveiled 50 years ahead of its time in London, when Joseph Paxton used the new technology in iron, steel, and glass to produce the Crystal Palace at the World's Fair of 1851. Quickly labeled Paxton's Greenhouse, it proved to be a turning point in architecture. It was lightweight, light inside, and simple to build. No applied decoration marred its straightforward structure, and it became a beautiful visual experience, featuring natural light and shadow. It was **symbolic** too, with a length of 1,851 feet to symbolize the year it was built.

The logo above is Frank Lloyd Wright's horizontally emphasized Prairie Style.

Four basic design approaches arose in the early 1900s: (1) Organic, (2) Mechanical, (3) Sculptural, and (4) Art Deco or Art Nouveau.

PERIOD OR STYLE	APPROXIMATE DATE	HOW TO RECOGNIZE IT (VISUAL CLUES)	DESCRIPTION
Twentieth Century	1851	 *22h.1.* **Crystal Palace, London; Paxton, 1851.**  *22h.2.* **Crystal Palace, exterior.**	*22h.1 and 22h.2.* Cast-iron girders and trusses, exposed as structure. Glass walls, ceiling. Impressionistic use of light and shadow. No ornamental decoration applied. The structure is expressed as its own decoration.
	1899	 *22h.3.* **Carson, Pirie, Scott Building, Chicago; Sullivan, 1899.**	*22h.3.* The steel skeleton is clearly shown and will later lead to skyscraper idea. Large areas of glass. No extraneous decoration of the building surfaces above the main floor. New height (12 stories); (Otis had invented the elevator). Sullivan coined the phrase, ''form follows function.''

PERIOD OR STYLE	APPROXIMATE DATE	HOW TO RECOGNIZE IT (VISUAL CLUES)	DESCRIPTION
Twentieth Century (cont'd.) Organic	1937	22h.4. **Falling Water, Bear Run, Pennsylvania; Frank Lloyd Wright, 1936-1939.**	22h.4. Materials harmonize with nature: wood used as wood, stone as stone, etc. Human scale. Forms harmonize with nature.
Mechanical	1952	22h.5. **School of Architecture and Design—Crown Hall, Illinois Institute of Technology, Chicago; Ludwig Mies van der Rohe, 1952.**	22h.5. Steel and glass boxes. Architecture is a "machine in which we live."
Sculptural	1950	22h.6. **Notre Dame du Haut, Ronchamp, France; Le Corbusier, 1950**	22h.6-22h.9. Concrete masses in more or less "free forms." Thick window openings placed visually rather than mechanically. Curvilinear decoration, including use of serpentine.

PERIOD OR STYLE	APPROXIMATE DATE	HOW TO RECOGNIZE IT (VISUAL CLUES)	DESCRIPTION
Art Deco	1930		22h.7-22h.10. Geometric linear decoration of surfaces.

22h.7.
Chrysler Building, New York City; Van Allen, 1930.

22h.8.
Chrysler Building, detail.

22h.9.
Chrysler Building, tower.

22h.10. **Tower of Waldorf Astoria Hotel, New York City; c. 1935.**

PERIOD OR STYLE	APPROXIMATE DATE	HOW TO RECOGNIZE IT (VISUAL CLUES)	DESCRIPTION
International	1924	 *22h.11.* **Schroeder house, Utrecht, Germany; Gerrit Rietveldt, 1924.**	The Mechanical Style evolved into the steel, concrete, and glass box and became known as the International Style. It began with Le Corbusier's blocky homes and offices and the Gropius's factories. It has climaxed in the steel-glass skyscraper. *22h.11.* Blocky slabs—very rectilinear (cubist). Studied proportions. No decoration on surfaces. Flat roof.
	1958	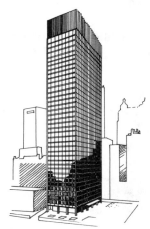 *22h.12.* **Seagram Building, New York City; Ludwig Mies van der Rohe and Philip Johnson, 1958.**	*22h.12.* Steel skeleton expressed. Glass box. No extraneous forms or decoration included in the design.
Summary Self Test	1907	 *22h.13.* **Casa Mila, Barcelona, Spain; Gaudi, 1907.**	In summary, the Organic Style may include extremes, such as Gaudi's Casa Mila in Barcelona (1907), which is also very sculptural, or Wright's desert residence—Taliesin West in Arizona (1938)—which harmonizes with the natural forms, colors, and textures of the desert. The mechanical styles arae "zenithed" by the Pompidou Center in Paris, where all parts are exposed as part of the design. Brightly colored pipes and vents, equipment, and glass are visible elements. The Art Nouveau Style shows up in older twentieth-century buildings. Often it is found in the older subway entries. *Figure 22h.17* is an interior from the old Hotel Van Dervelde in Brussels (1895). This idea persists as a statement against too-bland, inhumane "machine" concepts. The Sculptural architectural style shows up in many forms, mostly in concrete, but occasionally in tentlike forms of tension structures.

PERIOD OR STYLE	APPROXIMATE DATE	HOW TO RECOGNIZE IT (VISUAL CLUES)	HOW TO RECOGNIZE IT (VISUAL CLUES)

1938

22h.14. **Taliesin West, near Scottsdale, Arizona; Frank Lloyd Wright, 1938-1959.**

1977

22h.15. **Pompidou Center, Paris; Piano and Rogers, 1977.**

1895

22h.16. **Hotel Van Eetvelde, Brussels, Belgium; Victor Horta, 1895.**

1958

22h.17. **Palazzetto dello sport, Rome; Pier Luigi Nervi, 1958.**

1959

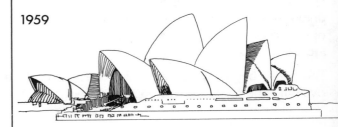

22h.18. **Sydney Opera House, Australia; Jorn Utzon, 1959-1973.**

1971

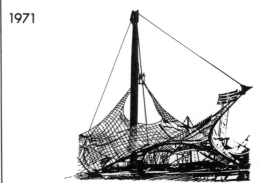

22h.19. **Olympic Stadium model, Munich, Germany; Frei Otto, 1971.**

Remember that styles and periods tend to change gradually. They do not switch from style "A" to style "B" on "the 17th of the month at five P.M." The periods in which change is evolving exhibit a metamorphosis which is often confusing when we are trying to identify a clear style or period. You may find perhaps *three* styles intertwined in any particular building.

Cognitive: From memory, quickly make a list of the major style periods in order.

When you have checked that list for accuracy, sketch a rough example of each style or period within the major categories, including in your sketches those key features by which a structure may be classified. Visual memory is very long staying, and sketching puts the characteristics into your visual memory.

Example: Egyptian (Early Dynasties)

Design "a church for factory workers." Do *not* use any past styles, but create totally unique forms which you've never seen before—something you think would be appropriate for the workers' spiritual meditation. Function and form should interrelate logically.

You might begin by making a list of styles and periods you will *not* be using. (By avoiding them, you prove your knowledge of them.)

CONCEPT

Architectural historians categorize classical buildings using "the orders" of architecture.

LESSON

"We are all Greeks." —Shelley

Much of our environment, buildings, art, and ways of thinking comes from classical Greece. Our laws, literature, religions, sculpture, and art, as well as classical government buildings, have their roots in Greece. Such important key words as *democracy, mythology, geometry,* and *philosophy* betray a Greek origin.

When you look at columns on homes, buildings, or monuments in your city, you can categorize them by looking at the tops of the columns, called the **capitals.** A simple capital is **Doric.** When it has rams' horns or scroll-like curls, it is **Ionic.** When it has acanthus leaves and looks detailed, it is **Corinthian.** If it has all of the above, it is a **Combination** or a **Composite.**

23.1.
Doric

23.2.
Ionic

23.3.
Corinthian

23.4.
Composite

B

You may see columns which have capitals different from the orders, such as the two in *figures 23.5 and 23.6.* They are useful for classification too.

Modern columns may be simple I post columns, or concrete rectangles *(fig. 23.7).*

The Greek orders also had a total nomenclature for the building parts to aid classification and recognition. *Figure 23.8* is an example of the Doric and Ionic part identities.

The most famous classical **ordered** building from history is the Parthenon. It is built on a hill called the Acropolis in Athens, Greece *(fig. 23.9).* The Parthenon has beautiful proportions. Can you tell which order the architects, Callicrates and Ictinus, selected for it? (The Romans simply copied the Greek orders and made a few variations.)

23.5.
Egyptian

23.6.
Byzantine or Christian

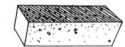

23.7.

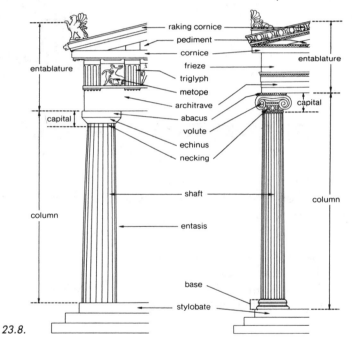

raking cornice
pediment
cornice
entablature
frieze
triglyph
metope
architrave
abacus
volute
echinus
necking
entablature
capital
capital
column
shaft
column
entasis
base
stylobate

23.8.

23.9. **The Parthenon, Athens, Greece; Callicrates and Ictinus, 432 B.C.**

PRODUCTIVE THINKING

Cognitive: Research to find and identify orders from pictures, diagrams, and in the community.

Divergent: Design a column order of your own. Make it *un*like others you have studied.

Visit community buildings with classical orders. Identify the revival orders they used.

4/24

Once the basic architectural periods and styles can be recognized, some unique labels can be used to categorize the homes and buildings in your own community.

The most useful tools of recognition are always the basic periods and styles like Greek, Roman, Romanesque, Gothic, Renaissance, and Baroque.

You may learn some special terms to deal with revivals, copies, and new styles in homes. The oldest examples are the Colonials.

PERIOD OR STYLE	APPROXIMATE DATE	HOW TO RECOGNIZE IT (VISUAL CLUES)	DESCRIPTION
Colonial Spanish	1600–1700	24.1.	24.1. Spanish stucco. Romanesque simplicity.
New England		24.2.	24.2. New England=stone, shingles, few windows.
Southern		24.3.	24.3. Narrow, steep gables (one room wide). Stepped gables. Brick, often in patterns. Massive chimneys with diagonal stacks. Some classical elements.

PERIOD OR STYLE	APPROXIMATE DATE	HOW TO RECOGNIZE IT (VISUAL CLUES)	DESCRIPTION
Colonial (cont'd.) French	1700-1830	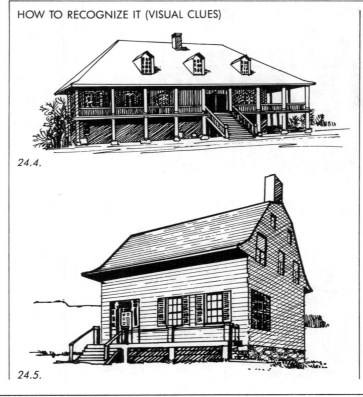 24.4.	24.4. Hip roof. Raised basement. Pavilion roof over porch with thin colonettes. French double casement windows. Exterior main staircase.
Eastern Dutch	1700-1800	24.5.	24.5. Gambrel (gable elaborated) roof system. Overhang from gambrel roof flare. Window shutters. Wide, horizontal board siding.
Georgian	1700-1800	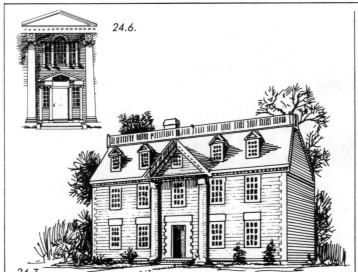 24.6. 24.7.	24.6. and 24.7. Classical entries and gables using pediments. Symmetrical. Colossal pilasters and columns. Palladian windows (Baroque and Mannerist). Transom lights above and to sides of doorway. From the time of King George in England. Quoins.

PERIOD OR STYLE	APPROXIMATE DATE	HOW TO RECOGNIZE IT (VISUAL CLUES)	DESCRIPTION
Classical Styles Georgian Federal	1780-1820	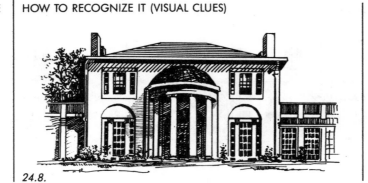 24.8.	24.8. Classical revival ideas. "Curved" Georgian (entries, windows, bays are curved or arched). Symmetrical. Basic box structure with classical entry.
Classicism Roman Greek	1790-1830	 24.9. 24.10.	24.9. Classical revival continues during these years. Steep Roman pediments. First floor has a "podium," as in Roman temples. 24.10. Pediments attached to basic box structure. Columns tall, slender.

PERIOD OR STYLE	APPROXIMATE DATE	HOW TO RECOGNIZE IT (VISUAL CLUES)	DESCRIPTION
Classicism (cont'd.) Greek (cont'd.)	1820-1860	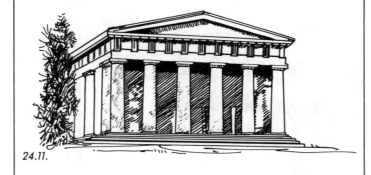 24.11.  24.12.	*24.11 and 24.12.* Low gable; pediment of Greek style. Classical Doric, Ionic, or Corinthian capitals. Low stylobate.

PERIOD OR STYLE	APPROXIMATE DATE	HOW TO RECOGNIZE IT (VISUAL CLUES)	DESCRIPTION
Egyptian Revival	1830-1850 1920-1930	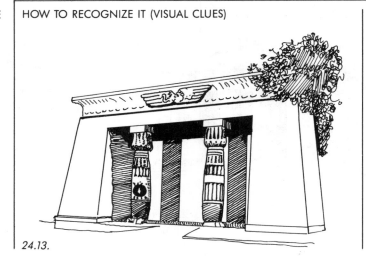 *24.13.*	*24.13.* Decorated ''lotus'' columns. Traditional Egyptian wing décor. Heavy, authoritarian look.
Gothic Revival	1830-1890	 *24.14.*	*24.14.* Pointed arches. Detailed cornice, roof lines. Steep roof gables. Building materials become decorative. Carpenter Gothic (carved fascia, pinnacles, and barge boards).

PERIOD OR STYLE	APPROXIMATE DATE	HOW TO RECOGNIZE IT (VISUAL CLUES)	DESCRIPTION
Victorian Italian Villa	1830-1880	 24.15.	*24.15.* One tall tower with subsidiary forms. Gables are gentle, pitched Classical pediments. Small, square windows on top floor. Grouped windows. Boxed-in bay windows. Round top Romanesque windows or entries. Wide bracketed cornice and eaves often have balustrade.
Italianate	1840-1880	24.16.	*24.16.* Boxlike structure. Large cornice of Renaissance palazzo. Low pitch hipped roof. Wide bracketed eaves. Windows often grouped in threes.
Renaissance Revival Early	1840-1890	24.17.	*24.17.* ''Formal'' looking. Windows have pediments and molded sill. Entry with pilaster (attached columns). Large cornices. Often a balustrade above. Often quoins.

PERIOD OR STYLE	APPROXIMATE DATE	HOW TO RECOGNIZE IT (VISUAL CLUES)	DESCRIPTION
Renaissance Revival (cont'd.) Later	1890-1920	 24.18.	*24.18.* Often an emphasis on Romanesque portion of the Renaissance (round arch). Large structures. Distinct horizontal layers (floor lines). Balustrade above cornice. Quoins.
Romanesque Revival Richardsonian	1840-1900	 24.19.  24.20.	*24.19 and 24.20.* Proportions blocky in stature. Round arch entries, windows. Towers topped with ''squatty''-proportioned pyramid.

PERIOD OR STYLE	APPROXIMATE DATE	HOW TO RECOGNIZE IT (VISUAL CLUES)	DESCRIPTION
Ecclectic (mixture of styles)	1850-1893	 24.21.  24.22.	*24.21 and 24.22.* Figure 24.21 has Romanesque details, Gothic ''feel,'' and Baroque-Rococo interior. Facade flanked by square towers. Fortress or castle details with battlements. Pyramidal tower roofs. Round-top windows (semicircular arch). Recognizable horizontal layers. Grouped Christian columns, usually quite short.

PERIOD OR STYLE	APPROXIMATE DATE	HOW TO RECOGNIZE IT (VISUAL CLUES)	DESCRIPTION
Victorian	1860-1890	**We entered the Victorian Period in horse-drawn carriages, but left it in model-T Fords. We went from fireplaces and wood stoves to ranges and furnaces, from privy to bathroom, from pump to hot and cold running water, with electric lights about to emerge. The Victorian Period may very well be our most versatile and creative period— uninhibited, expressive, and innovative.**	**The villa concepts introduced a general style we call Victorian. It dates from Queen Victoria in 1837, until 1901. ''Victorian'' includes French Chateau Victorian, Victorian Italianate, Victorian Gothic, Victorian Elizabethan, Victorian Ecclectic (using several combinations of styles), Victorian Eastlake, Victorian Queen Anne, Victorian Romanesque, Victorian Shingled Villa, Victorian Colonial-Salt Box, Victorian Colonial, and Victorian Edwardian.**

Chateau

(later the Beaux
Arts Mansions,
1890-95)

24.23.

24.24.

24.23 and 24.24. From France, usually having large, two-story roofs—often mansard—with towers and tall chimneys.

Hipped or mansard roof.

Towers with conical roof.

Renaissance entries with semicircular arch.

Cross windows.

Balustrated roof cresting.

Renaissance, Gothic, and Baroque wall surface decoration.

PERIOD OR STYLE	APPROXIMATE DATE	HOW TO RECOGNIZE IT (VISUAL CLUES)	DESCRIPTION
Victorian (cont'd.) Second Empire	1860-1890	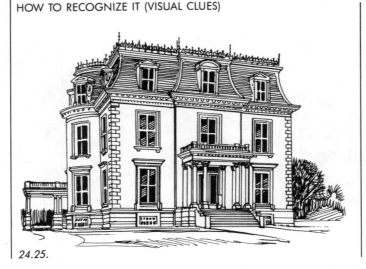 24.25.	*24.25.* Two to three stories with projecting proportions. Mansard roof. Classical mouldings and details with quoins, cornices, etc. Windows arched and with pediments; windows often paired in twos. Tall first floor windows. Tower's masonry ends at same level as rest of building, but roof usually taller.
Stick Style Eastern or Eastlake	1860-1890s	 24.26.	*24.26.* Spinning off of Gothic Revival styles, it emphasized applied carpenter decoration, and asymmetrical composition. Steep gable roof and cross gables. Large towers and pointed dormer gables. Similar to Gothic Revival forms. "Half timber" look with boards and cross-boards. Gable fascia rather ornate.

PERIOD OR STYLE	APPROXIMATE DATE	HOW TO RECOGNIZE IT (VISUAL CLUES)	DESCRIPTION
Victorian (cont'd.) Stick Style (cont'd.) Western (also called the "Wood Bungalow Residential" style)	1890-1920	 24.27.	24.27. Oriental influence. Organic feeling. Large overhangs and porches with ornamented structural corner posts. Struts or diagonal bracing. Western style more horizontal or spreading than Eastern.
Eastlake	1970-1890	 24.28.	24.28. Asymmetrical. A major gable protrudes and balances a tower of octagonal plan that contains windows. Decorative carved woodwork. Massive posts, turned on lathes. Spindle and lattice balustrade. Roof combined gable and hip. "Furniturelike" décor—rows of small knobs on banisters, etc. Ornamentation not sawed, but carved and turned on lathe. Rambling veranda. Balconies. Bay windows. Towers and gables.

PERIOD OR STYLE	APPROXIMATE DATE	HOW TO RECOGNIZE IT (VISUAL CLUES)	DESCRIPTION
Victorian (cont'd.) Shingle Style (Queen Anne style is similar)	1880-1900	 24.29.	*24.29.* Very large gable roofs. Shingle wall siding. Multi-gabled. Large porches. Tall chimneys.
Edwardian	1880-1900	 24.30.	*24.30.* Asymmetrical. Wide variety of forms. Variety of textures, colors. Towers, turrets, tall chimneys, pavilions, porches, bays, and encircling veranda porches or portico. Horizontal floors or layers of stone or brick; second story shingle or frame; top story may be stick or half timber. Cast-iron cresting on roof is often present. Fountainlike finial on top of towers or gables.

PERIOD OR STYLE	APPROXIMATE DATE	HOW TO RECOGNIZE IT (VISUAL CLUES)	DESCRIPTION
Neoclassicism	1900-1920	 24.31.	*24.31.* Classical pediment entries. First story often more "rustic" or fortresslike. Main floor has semicircular arch windows. Some windows grouped in pairs or triplets. Two to four stories. Classical cornice. Above cornice line, a frieze area (entablature). Appearance of flat roof. Colossal size columns.
Bungalow Style	1890-1940	 24.32.	*24.32-24.34.* A gabled or hipped roof facing street. Brick walls and porch in solid, non-decorated approach. Collar beams and rafters exposed. Wide window openings. Often a sun porch. Small windows flanking chimney. Usually dormer windows of some kind.

PERIOD OR STYLE	APPROXIMATE DATE	HOW TO RECOGNIZE IT (VISUAL CLUES)	DESCRIPTION
Bungalow Style (cont'd.)	1890-1940		

24.33.

24.34.

The California Bungalow style of Greene and Greene was very ''organic'' in feel. Frank Lloyd Wright's Bungalow style was more ''horizontal,'' and is called ''Prairie.''

PERIOD OR STYLE	APPROXIMATE DATE	HOW TO RECOGNIZE IT (VISUAL CLUES)	DESCRIPTION
Prairie Style (Extended Bungalow)	1900-1920	 24.35.	*24.35.* Horizontal lines. Brick and stucco. Bungalow look. Gabled and hipped roofs and projecting eaves. A raised, dominating form, either sunroom or chimney (centralized fireplace). Continuous line of windows. Horizontal tiers of walls in yard and house. Cantilevered roof.
Bauhaus Styles International, to Art Moderne, to Mies van der Rohe's steel/glass Universal Style) "Art Moderne" form of International	1920-1945, to present	 24.36.	*24.36 and 24.37.* Geometric and Mechanical. Harsh or crisp lines. Very white. No cornices or eaves. Flat roof. Curtain wall of glass. Smooth wall surfaces. Cantilevered balconies. No applied ornament. Clerestory windows. Lightweight structure. Cubist forms. Asymmetrical.

PERIOD OR STYLE	APPROXIMATE DATE	HOW TO RECOGNIZE IT (VISUAL CLUES)	DESCRIPTION
Bauhaus Styles (cont'd.) "Art Moderne" form of International	1920-1945	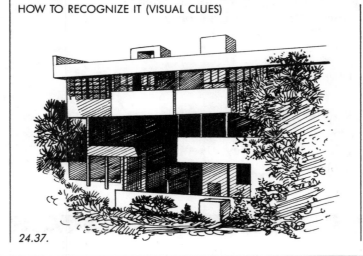 24.37.	
Art Deco	1925-1940	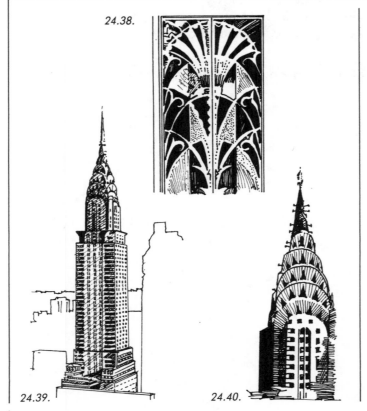 24.38. 24.39.　24.40.	*24.38-24.40.* Linear, angular, zig-zag ornamentation (decorative). **After World War II, the styles are variations of the Organic, Sculptural, and Machine styles (International). See lessons 7/48-49.**

If you are beginning to find "grey areas" in identifying styles and periods, even occasionally feeling confused, you are becoming visually literate. Professionals often wrestle with classification, too, and have come to realize that architects made their designs without considering whether or not they would fit cleanly and clearly into a precise style classification. So "bravo!" for you.

Following are some exercises relative to what you have learned about identifying architecture.

Cognitive: Identify all of the influences from past styles or periods in your own home or apartment building. *Example:* The side lights by my door are Georgian. The porch columns are Classic Revival, in this case, Greek in origin. The chimney is centered at the end of the gable as in English-Dutch Gothic homes, etc.

Identify styles in your community and/or state.

Divergent: Create a *new style* for a home's facade. This must be your own unique idea. Do not use anything from the past. Make a list of obvious things you cannot use, such as: gables, cornices, traditional doors, side lights, classical columns or pediments, traditional windows, traditional chimneys, and so on. Go to work, and discover how tradition-bound we are as designers.

Organize, or become involved in, an architectural preservation association, such as your local history group or heritage foundation.

CONCEPT

Forms may be convex or concave. They occupy space and create space.

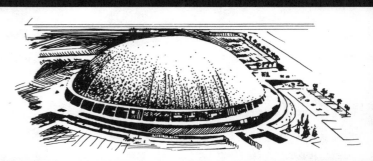

LESSON

Convex forms bulge outward, like the exterior of a sphere. 25.1.

Concave forms curve inward, like the interior of a sphere. 25.2.

So while a convex **positive** form is created, a concave **negative** space exists under it or to its side or within it. 25.3.

In a cup, a liquid can fill the negative space.

Here is a doubly convex form. 25.4.

Here is a doubly concave form. 25.5.

Architects use such forms to plan their buildings. *Figure 25.6* shows the government buildings at Brasilia, a rather new city, built on a site in the jungle and chosen to be the capital city of Brazil.

25.6.
Government buildings at Brasilia, Brazil; Lucio de Costa, c. 1955.

F

Look at the buildings in *figures 25.7 through 25.9.* Does each building with a **convex** form also have a **concave** form? Explain this concept. (The opposite form is present, but not necessarily exposed to view.)

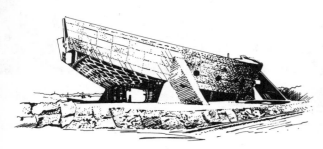

25.7.
Kagawa Gymnasium, Takamatsu, Japan; Kenzo, Tange, and Associates, 1966.

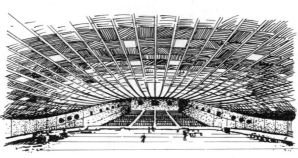

25.8.
Kagawa Gymnasium interior.

25.9.
U.S. Pavilion, Montreal; Buckminster Fuller, 1967.

See *figures 25.10 through 25.11.* Have these buildings used convex or concave form? How?

25.10.
Legislative Assembly Building, Chandigarh Capitol Complex, India; Le Corbusier, 1961-64.

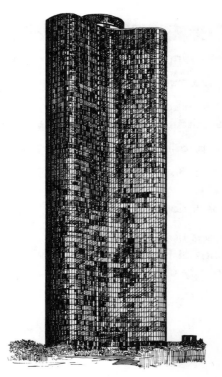

25.11.
Lake Point Tower, Chicago; Schipporeit-Heinrich, Inc., 1968.

Have you ever noticed that a container, such as a cup or a bottle, can force liquids or solids to take its particular form? This is best seen by filling half of a rubber ball with plaster. When the plaster has set, it is the shape of the inside of the ball. The inside of the ball is convex, but the plaster form is the shape of the space it encloses. One affects the other. What are all of the convex things you can list? All of the concave things?

Analogy: Convex is to concave as _____ is to _____.

(Outer shell, inner space; explode, collapse.) One example of your own?

Cognitive/Convergent: Make a drawing of a convex and a concave shape, from memory or imagination.

Divergent: Create either a convex or a concave form (crayons, plaster, or construction materials may be used) which has a new and unusual use. *(Figure 25.12 is a typical example.)*

Create a building which uses both convex and concave forms.

25.12.
A ruler which doesn't "smudge."

4/26

Variations in the elements can make space divisions more interesting.

Variety or diversity is an important design consideration because "too much" visual activity may cause a **chaotic** effect. On the other hand, no variety or diversity results in **monotony.** The architectural designer must walk the tightrope between chaos and boredom to create a building or space of enticing interest.

The old architectural design adage, "Less is more and more is less," has encountered a new adage which says simply, "Less is boring." Thus the two philosophies, at different ends of this conceptual spectrum, describe the importance of the principle.

At one end of the spectrum, with very little diversity, we might find the Seagram Building in New York City *(fig. 26.1)*— simply a grid/glass box. Its real diversity is in its simple contrast with the surrounding "cityscape" and the reflections of that cityscape on its mirrorlike glass sides. Its harmonious colors and proportions make it a work of art.

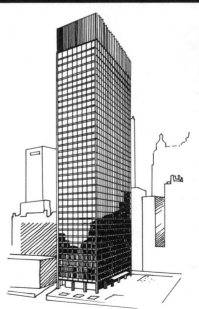

26.1.
Seagram Building, New York; Ludwig Mies van der Rohe and Philip Johnson, 1958.

G

At the other end of the **variety** spectrum we might find a Japanese pagoda *(fig. 26.2)*, or a building such as the Einstein Tower, Potsdam, by Eric Mendelsohn *(fig. 26.3)*.

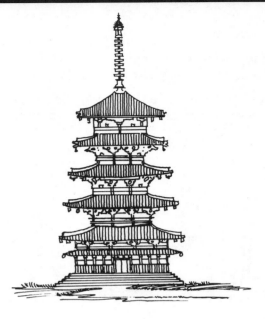

26.2.
Horyu-ji Pagoda, Nara, Japan; originally A.D. 607.

26.3.
Einstein Tower, Potsdam, Germany; Erich Mendelsohn, 1919.

It is interesting that nature uses a very subtle variation of elements which create such interesting forms. Often we think of the leaves on a tree as being all exactly alike, when in reality each one is unique.

In Le Corbusier's proposed design for a building in Algiers, 1938 *(fig. 26.4)*, we see a radial design used to give variety— each view being unique, yet each still in the same pattern and each wing nearly exactly like its "triplet."

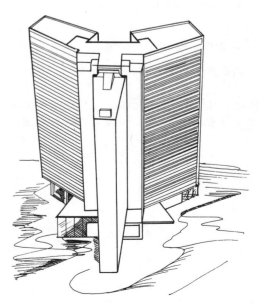

26.4.
Proposed design for Algiers, never built; Le Corbusier, 1938.

In the facade in *figure 26.5,* the rhythm has little variation and few surprises. It is predictable.

In the other facade *(fig. 26.6),* the rhythm has more variety, but the detail makes perception of the **basic** rhythm less obvious.

When sketching a fenceline *(fig. 26.7),* an artist often "tips" a post, or joins two together, just to break the regular monotony.

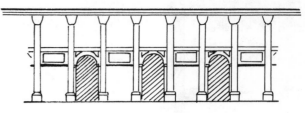

26.5.

26.6.

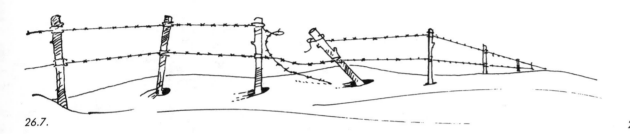

26.7.

When the building has no variety it is _____. (Stale, sterile, boring, too plain, boxy, etc.)

When a building has too much variety it is _____.

What are some ways to make a group of squares have variety? 26.8.

What are all of the images you can make which will "force" the viewer to think "square"? *(See fig. 26.9 for some typical responses.)*

$$\left(SQUARE, \ \square, \ \square, \ \underset{(TOWN\ SQUARE)}{\text{🏘}}, \ \text{😊}, \ \llcorner, \ \vdash, \ x^2, \ \sqrt{} \ \right)$$

26.9.

Cognitive: Find a picture of a house or a building. Trace it and change it to have either more or less variety.

Divergent: If you had to make a long facade on a building, how would you vary the elements to make sure it was interesting to look at? What are all of the things you might vary? (Doors, windows, lines, colors, textures, forms, roof lines, etc.)

Using the facade in *figure 26.10,* add a variety of elements without having it lose its unity and become chaotic, and be careful not to make it so simple that it is boring to look at. You may want to change the roof, indent entries, create arcades, use landscape, change heights, and so on. The vanishing points are shown to help you draw the changes.

Consider the need for variety in lifestyles (hobbies, sports, food, vacations, etc.). What are the areas of your life which ought to have more variety?

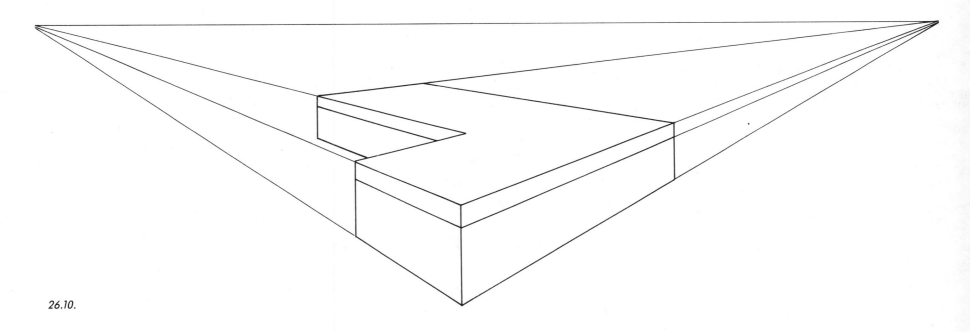

26.10.

Divide the square in *figure 26.11* into four equal sections—equal in **area** and identical in **shape.**

26.11.

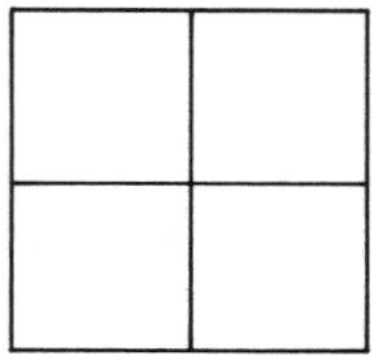

26.12.
**Did it look
like this?**

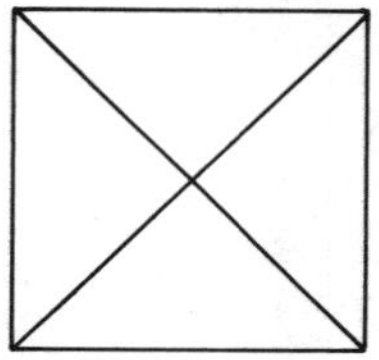

26.13.
Or this?

What other ways can you divide a square into four equal parts?
Use the squares in *figure 26.14* for practice.

26.14.

Concept 1: A square may be divided into equal fourths by dividing the square into sixteen smaller squares, then putting the small squares together, four at a time, to make swastika shapes, **L** shapes, **T** shapes, diagonals, and so on. *(Fig. 26.15 shows some examples.)*

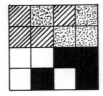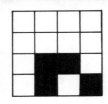

26.15.
Visual example   **Basic shape used**

Now can you improve on some of those you tried earlier?

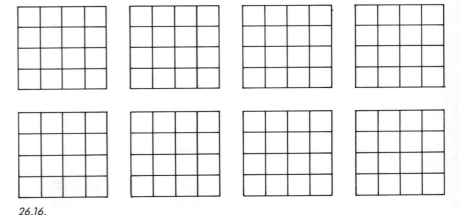

26.16.

Concept 2: Any line which passes from a point on the edge of the square to an equivalent point on the opposite edge has the same shape on both sides of center, and divides the square in half. Each of those halves can be divided into equal halves by repeating the process at 90°, or by simply creating equivalent shapes with each half.

Using this concept, how many ways can you divide these squares into four equal sections?

26.17.

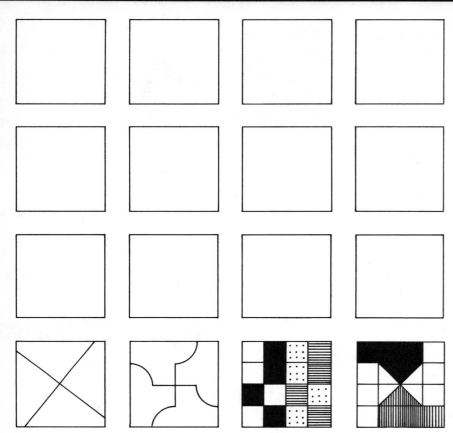

26.18.
Some typical responses:

4/27

Symbolism is an important part of many architectural designs. It is one way buildings "talk" to us.

What is a symbol? (A symbol is an image which communicates to others an idea of something.) Words are just symbols. If you see or hear the word **rose,** you get an image in your mind. This is the word's **meaning.** What color of rose did you have in mind? Was it a bud, in full bloom, or a bush? Was it fragrant? Some aesthetic philosophers distinguish between "sign" and "symbol." (A symbol represents another idea or an abstraction. A sign indicates a "thing.")

Pictures and sculpture may be symbolic, yet they are not words. Can you tell what the symbols in *figure 27.1* mean?

Musical symbols *(fig. 27.2)* help us to play and interpret with our voices or instruments.

Visual symbols cause us to react in a particular way. A cross ✝ , a flag , the Star of David ✡ , the dove , a swastika 卍 , or even a flashing red light ☀ may cause us to **behave** in certain ways. How do crowds at a parade behave when the country's flag is passing by?

27.1.

27.2.

J

Divergent: List all of the symbols you can think of. (Wise owl, royal lion, royal blue, kelly green, angry red, Nazi swastika, dove of peace, Christian cross, Yin/Yang opposition, crossed bones—poison, etc.)

What are all of the religious symbols you can think of? Company (business) symbols? Logos?

Draw as many symbols as you can which will cause someone to think "light."

Similes: Symbols are important in similes such as "green as grass," "solid as rock (or Gibraltar)," "wise as an owl," "innocent as a lamb," and "strong as an ox." You see why grass can be symbolized by green. Why does a lamb symbolize innocence?

Make up several symbol words for this simile: As quiet as _____. (A mouse, snow falling, the wind, a cloud, time passing.)

Divergent: Humpty Dumpty is a visual example of a familiar symbol which is both complex and simple. Simply, he can be the symbol for the fragility of an egg. In a more complex understanding, he can sit on the wall precariously symbolizing pride and the inevitable fall. He can even stand for the fall of Adam, or Icarus.

Two professors found these symbols *(fig. 27.3)* on a wall of a cave in the Pyrenees Mountains. One professor thought they were ancient hieroglyphs. The other professor said, "No, they are obviously not ancient hieroglyphs!" What did he see which the other professor did not see? (He saw the number symbols 1, 2, 3, 4 and 5, and their mirrored images.) Could you make up the image for the numbers 6 and 7?

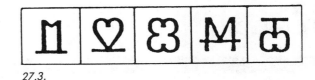

27.3.

What do you think would happen if a stop sign shape said "go" on it *(fig. 27.4)*? (Many people would stop because the **visual** symbol is often stronger and more emphatic than **word** symbols.)

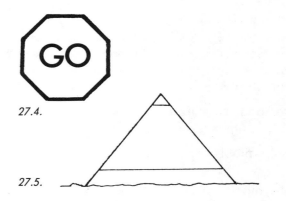

27.4.

Buildings may be symbols, or their walls, windows, and doors may be decorated with symbols. Statham, an architectural critic and author said, "All architecture—that is, all that is worth the name—is one vast symbolism."

The pyramid is a symbol of Egypt's government, with pharaoh at the top point and the people under the crushing weight at the bottom *(fig. 27.5)*.

27.5.

The ancient domed Stūpa of India *(fig. 27.6)* symbolized the canopy of heaven. This idea was also symbolized in early Turkish domes like Hagia Sophia *(fig. 27.7)*.

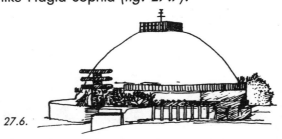

27.6.

27.7.

In the great cathedrals of the Gothic Period, the large rose window *(fig. 27.8)* symbolized the sun and light, which symbolized Christ as the light of the world. Its circular, wheel-like shape symbolized eternity as "one infinite round." It also symbolized the eye of God and the wheel of fortune discussed by Ezekiel in the Old Testament (Ezekiel, Chapter 1).

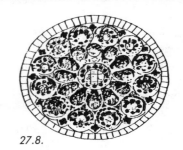

27.8.

The columns of the cathedral *(fig. 27.9)* have been said by some to symbolize a heavenly forest to hold up the sky canopy, and emphasize looking upward. The cathedral's floor plan is a cross to symbolize Christianity *(fig. 27.10)*.

The pioneer buildings of Temple Square in Salt Lake City, Utah, symbolize the eternal family—the purpose for every Mormon Temple. There are many other important symbols at Temple Square—among them the Star of David, the Angel Moroni *(fig. 27.14)*, "earth stones" *(fig. 27.15)*, sun stones, moon stones, star stones *(fig. 27.16)*, cloud stones *(fig. 27.17)*, and spire stones.

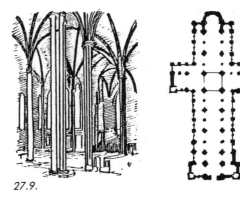

27.9.   *27.10.*

27.11.
Mormon Temple, Salt Lake City, Utah, U.S.A.; Truman Angel, 1893.

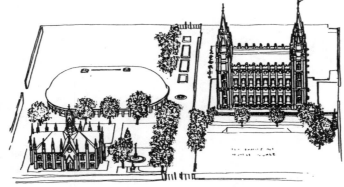

27.12.

27.13.

27.14.   *27.15.*

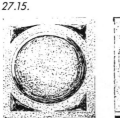
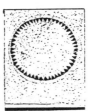
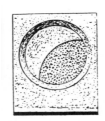

27.16.   *27.17.*

The old "Chrisman Symbol" was used to stand for Christianity before the cross was used. It looks like this ✗ and symbolized Christ. "Chi" (χ) and "Rho" (ρ) were Christ's monogram. Further, the "Chi" is a cross, and the "Rho" is a shepherd's staff. Now you see that many symbols help buildings to speak to us.

SUGGESTED ACTIVITIES

1. Design a symbol for your front door. It should symbolize something important to you and those who live in your house.

2. Design a symbol for yourself, symbolizing something about you which is different from others.

3. Visit a nearby church and study its structure to find symbols.

5/28

An understanding of proportion helps an architect to arrange the forms more aesthetically.

LESSON

It has been said that the most important and difficult mental control in design is the judgement of proportion. The goal of all theories of proportion is to create a sense of **order** among design elements. The skill of judging proportion requires the assessment of the proportional relationship between two rectangles *(fig. 28.1)*. The simplest way to do this is to superimpose one upon the other *(fig. 28.2)*. Rather than actually measuring or counting, one can **sense** the relationship (the small is about 40%) by **eye.**

The human body is full of marvelous proportional relationships. Look at your own hands to see an excellent example. Notice how finger joints fit into indentations on the other finger *(fig. 28.3)*. Notice that the first knuckle section is only half of the largest knuckle section *(fig. 28.4)*. The middle section is about 1½ first sections.

These are proportional relationships, and buildings require the same beautiful relationships.

28.1. **This to that** 28.2.

OR

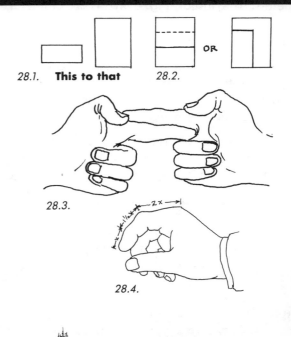

28.3.

28.4.

E

Does the designer make a room cubical or oblong, low or high, or does he make a tall, impressive facade? How does the designer decide? The easy part of the decision comes from materials, function, and costs. For example, certain materials only come in specific sizes or strengths. If the designer wants a long span of beam, a big, heavy stone would not be wise. A thick wood beam, steel **I**-beam, or truss would be better. (Stone is not strong in **tension,** but it is in **compression.**)

A low ceiling would not be a wise choice if the room's **function** were to be for indoor tennis.

Thus, many decisions are almost obvious and immediate. The difficult problem is to find the beautiful or **appropriate** proportional relation.

A proportioning system establishes a consistent set of visual relationships between the parts of a building and the whole building. One of those systems you will learn about is the **golden mean**—a specific geometric proportion (Lesson 5/29). Another system is **the orders** (Lesson 4/23). The orders are so labeled because the height of a column was determined by the size of the building and column spacing, with column diameter as the measure. This Corinthian example *(fig. 28.5)* shows column height to be 8⅓ diameters. The Tuscan *(fig. 28.6)* is six diameters tall.

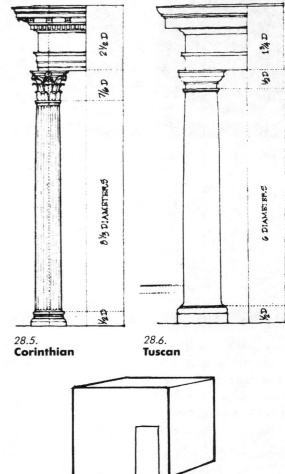

28.5.
Corinthian

28.6.
Tuscan

Another system architects have used, based on numerical or mathematical harmonies, is, for instance, that during the Renaissance an architect would determine room height (ceilings) by rules such as this: A flat-roofed room should have a ceiling height equal to the width of the room *(fig. 28.7)*.

There is another proportioning system based on the **human body.** This makes sense, since humans are to live in and use the building. Corbusier is a twentieth-century architect who uses this system, as well as the golden mean *(fig. 28.8)*.

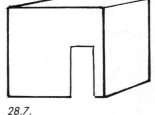

28.7.

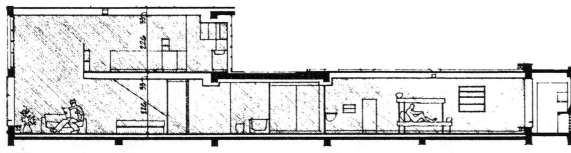

28.8.

Analogy: The essence of proportion is like an analogy. An analogy says, "This is to that as something else is to another." (Shoe is to foot as hat is to head.) Proportion says essentially the same thing. It may say, "Distance A is to Distance B as Distance B is to Distance C." Proportion is **analogical.**

Divergent: *Figure 28.9* is a Renaissance building. Can you identify a proportional system? (It is three times the distance from stylobate top to architrave tops, and it is about twice as high as its two widths—outer and inner.)

How many images can you make which would make someone think about proportion? *(See fig. 28.10.)*

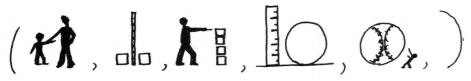

28.10.

28.9.
Tempietto S. Pietro, Rome; Donate Bramante, 1502.

What is the difference between **scale** and **proportion?** (Basically, scale deals with size, while proportion deals with relationships.) In perception of scale we use a familiar unit of comparison to the building or part. It is a measurement of comparative difference. The size of each element is seen relative to the sizes of other elements around it. In perception of **proportion,** the relationship is generally mathematical and relates to parts within the same whole. It is **size,** but measured against a mental norm or other elements.

Cognitive: Select any object in the room, or the room itself, and identify a proportional relationship. (So many widths tall, so many heads tall per person, height to length or width, and so on.) Everything has proportions, but some are more aesthetically pleasing than others. In the Renaissance proportional rule that a flat-roofed room should be the same height as its width, the result is that the "end walls" will always be a particular shape *(fig. 28.11)*. Do you see which shape that is?

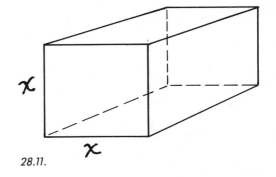

28.11.

Divergent: Create a design (or three-dimensional construction) which purposely has some part of the composition **out of proportion.** In *figure 28.12* the big rectangle or wall is so large that it overwhelms both the little rectangle (fireplace) and the line of carved decoration. Beginners may put size, shape, or attention-getting color out of proportion.

You may want to discuss ''problems'' as a subject. Sensitivity to proportional relationships pervades everything we see, think, or do. ''Making a mountain out of a molehill'' is an example of proportion, and describes someone's inability to see relationships as they really are. It is sociological as well as aesthetic.

Recipes are almost totally proportional in terms of cups, teaspoons, and so on.

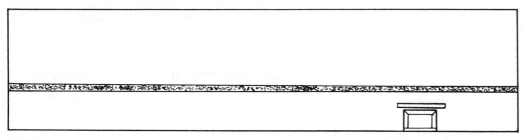

28.12.

5/29

CONCEPT

The golden mean is an historical concept used over the centuries to design buildings to a specific pleasing proportion.

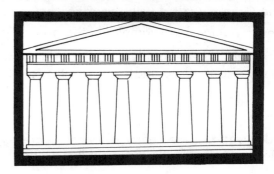

LESSON

The ancient Greeks were idealists and rationalists. These ideas made them feel that they were able to improve upon nature and that the human power to think is our greatest strength. They wanted buildings to be in **perfect** order, and decided that geometry was the way to make those buildings perfect. As they sought for the perfect rectangle, they began with a square *(fig. 29.1)*.

They put a compass point at the mid-point of the base of the square, stretched the compass to the upper corner, and swung an arc *(fig. 29.2)*.

When they extended the square's base line to meet the compass line, they found that they could make a beautifully proportioned rectangle *(fig. 29.3)*. They called this the **golden proportion** or **golden rectangle** or **golden mean** or **golden section.**

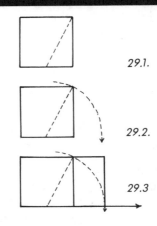

29.1.

29.2.

29.3

G

They designed their beautiful Parthenon using that proportion. (The proportion is 1:1.6 and any multiples. Notice that if you multiply by 3, the relationship comes very close to 3 by 5.) The Parthenon is the logo illustration for the concept above, showing how it fits such a rectangle.

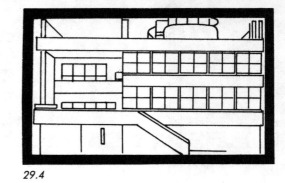

29.4

In the twentieth century, Le Corbusier has used the golden rectangle for this home *(fig. 29.4)* outside of Paris. It fits within such a 3 by 5 shape.

As the Greeks worked with this ratio, they also discovered that proportion exists many places in nature. For example, in the original golden rectangle,  the new rectangle on the right is also "golden." If the original square is taken away, the "new" smaller shape is also golden, and so on almost to infinity, until too small to see.

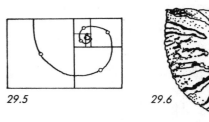

If a dot is put at the center of each square *(fig. 29.5)*, the dots can be connected to create a **spiral,** like that in a shell *(fig. 29.6)*.

29.5   29.6

Some pine trees apparently grow at this same rate and proportion, with the top branches being ⅗ shorter than the second row of branches, and so on down the tree *(fig. 29.7)*.

29.7

The pentagram (five-pointed star) is created from a group of line segments related by the golden proportion *(fig. 29.8)*.

The effort to design aesthetic proportion (harmony of parts to the whole) is essentially **qualitative,** not quantitative. Today, aesthetic proportions are mostly arrived at "by eye" or intuition of an experienced designer. Many designers feel that numerical, quantitative approaches are actually illogical, because the eye, in reality, sees **relationships,** not measurement.

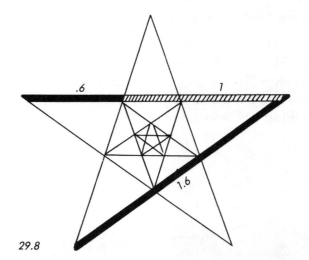

29.8

Divergent: In the optical illusion using circles *(fig. 29.9)*, which center circle is larger? (They are the same.) The small circles around the center make the middle circle *appear* to be larger. The relationship, which is unmeasured, depends more on the eye than on numbers.

Similes: Proportions are like _____. Why?

The golden proportion is as beautiful as _____.

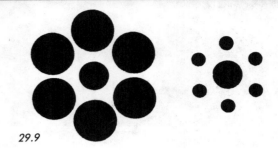

29.9

Cognitive: Create a golden rectangle using ruler and compass *(fig. 29.10)*. Measure the length and height.

Divergent: Make a design, using various colors of construction paper which is cut into golden rectangles and squares *(fig. 29.11)*. Make the overall piece of paper a golden rectangle too.

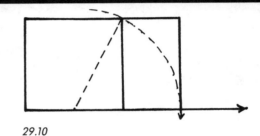

29.10

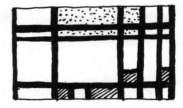

29.11

5/30

Buildings can be designed to meet the requirements of people with special needs.

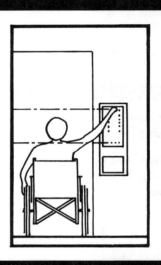

One of the finest courses an architect can take is Architectural Psychology or Designing **for People.**

In the lessons on proportion and scale (lessons 2/12, 3/18, 5/28, 7/47) we find that one of the basic proportional systems is based on the human body (anthropomorphic). However, true architectural creativity in planning scale and proportion comes with the realization that an "average" human body does not really exist. There are babies, children, all sizes of grown-ups, and handicapped persons. They all vary in age, sex, and needs. The proportions of our sizes to the world around us affect what we handle, eat and drink, and the distance we can reach *(fig. 30.1)*. Our needs to sit, work, eat, eliminate waste, and sleep must be considered and designed into our spaces.

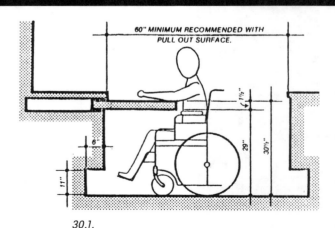

60" MINIMUM RECOMMENDED WITH PULL OUT SURFACE.

30.1.

K

What are all of the problems young children might encounter in a building? (Doors too heavy, sinks or toilets too high, towels out of reach, light switches or elevator buttons too high, signs too hard to read, etc.)

They are in the same predicament as someone in a wheelchair *(fig. 30.2)*. What are all of the extra problems you would have if *you* were in a wheel chair?

Let's test your visual memory. Draw the international symbol (no words) for "handicapped." Then look at *figure 30.3* to check your memory.

Did you know there are also symbols for "deaf," "blind," and *both* "deaf and blind"? Before seeing these symbols, how would you create a sign everyone would understand *(draw inside the squares in figs. 30.4 through 30.6)*. Architects must plan such symbols into their buildings so that people understand those special functions.

In what places might handicapped people want such signs to guide them? (Rest rooms with special facilities, tables made for wheel chairs, ramps, hearing aid hook-ups, parking, elevators, offices of people who understand sign language, etc.)

How could the streets in your city be altered to help the handicapped?

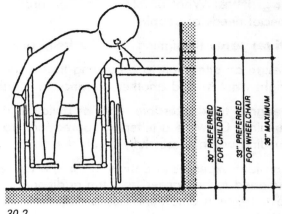

30.2.

30.3.
International sign for handicapped.

30.4.
Deaf

30.5.
Blind

30.6.
Deaf and blind

Cognitive: What problems does an architect create if the designs do not consider special needs of people?

Divergent: (Designing "barrier free" buildings.)

Design an alteration to a building that is now inaccessible to the handicapped. (You might want to add another entrance or modify the one now in use.)

Design a fully accessible room or building. It can be a school, store, church, office building. Or write a letter of appreciation to the owner, architect, and builder of a building which successfully meets the needs of special cases.

Consider expenses in designing for special needs. Studies show that if buildings are designed to be barrier free, the additional cost is about $\frac{1}{10}$ of one percent of the entire cost. This was determined by a national study made by the National League of Cities.

The cost of remodeling buildings is sometimes very high, but many times minimal changes can be used, yet help greatly.

ALTERNATE ACTIVITY

Go downtown and listen to the bells which ring to tell blind people it is safe to cross the street. If your community has none, find out why.

LEVEL 7 ACTIVITY
5/31

Light and shadow are an important solution to the world energy crisis.

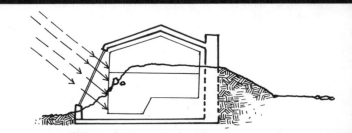

Light and shadow not only help us to perceive form and texture, but they keep us comfortable as well. Have you ever worn dark blue or black clothing out into the sunshine? It quickly warms up. The dark colors hold in the sun's rays. If your car sits in a parking lot in the sun, how does it feel when you get in? Have you ever played with a magnifying glass in the middle of the day *(fig. 31.1)*? A little magnifying lens can generate so much heat that it can burn paper, or even *you,* yet it requires no gasoline or electricity. It only uses the sun's rays. These experiences teach us that the sun is a marvelous source of clean energy. We are just beginning to learn how to use such a marvelous source of energy in our homes and buildings.

The logo above is a side view, sectional diagram of a house which allows sunlight to come through its big south windows. It is an "envelope-passive solar energy" home, because it has **walls** within its outside walls. There is an airspace wrapped all around the "inner house" like an envelope around a letter. The air which is warmed by the sun rises, goes up over the ceiling and down behind the rooms. As it goes *under* the inner house, the air cools and is drawn back into the sunny room by the rising air. It is very simple, very efficient, and requires no electricity, gas, or oil for heat. This house also has earth piled up around most of it for thick insulation. Down in the earth, even in cold wintry climates, it is still 57° (13.8° C.). Such homes are not only very comfortable, but very quiet. The earth insulates against noise as well as temperature extremes.

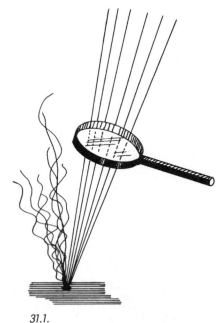

31.1.

L

There are many examples of solar energy buildings, but most fall into one of two main categories. These categories are **passive** and **active.** Active solar systems require more money and more energy than passive systems.

Active systems are divided into either **liquid** or **air** categories. They must use either pumps and pipes for liquid, or fans and ducts for air. The sun's energy rays are collected on dark panels which heat up water or air *(fig. 31.2.).* The water or air is then pumped or pushed onto a second set of dark panels, heating up water or air inside those panels. The water or air is then pumped or pushed into rooms in the house. With liquid (water) systems, the warm water must be stored in either water bags or a sort of "swimming pool" until needed on cloudy days or at night *(fig. 31.3.).*

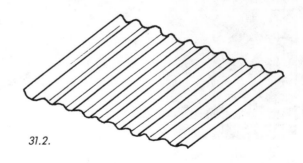

31.2.

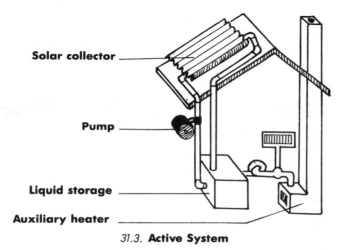

Solar collector

Pump

Liquid storage

Auxiliary heater

31.3. **Active System**

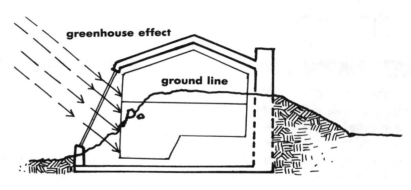

greenhouse effect

ground line

31.4. **Passive System**

Passive solar systems are designed so that no pumps or fans are required. The **natural** flow of heat is used. A backup source of heat may be as simple as a centralized wood-burning stove *(fig. 31.4.).*

Figures 31.5 and 31.6 are examples of some solar energy homes.

31.5.

31.6.

If natural gas, oil, gasoline, and electricity were too scarce or completely gone, what are all of the things which might happen? (Automobiles would stop, buildings would be without heat, elevators would quit, food would be difficult to transport, garbage would pile up—no trucks to collect it—, people would become uncomfortable, etc.)

What are all of the ways you can think of to get along without natural gas, oil, gasoline, and electricity? (Self-powered generators like the bicycle system on "Gilligan's Island," wood, coal, wind, water, sun, magnetism.)

SUGGESTED ACTIVITIES

Cognitive: Write a list of the reasons people are not rushing out to build solar homes.

Write down all of the things you could teach people to get them to be more excited about solar homes.

Divergent: Design your own solar home, just for you. Does it turn to follow the sun? Is it round?

Use a magnifying glass, outdoors, to focus the sun's rays and burn or scorch a piece of paper.

Visit a solar energy building near your home or in the community. You may have to call an architect to find the location of one.

5/32

The triangle is a shape which has great strength. It gives a feeling of stability to a design.

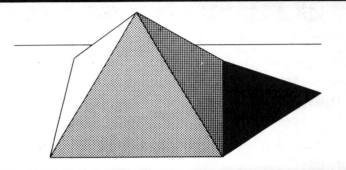

How many triangular things can you name *(figs. 32.1 and 32.2)*? (Tents, caution signs, roof gable, pine trees, etc.)

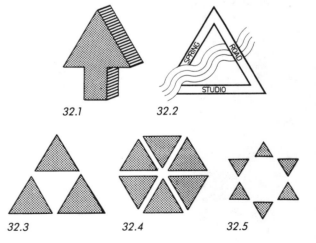

32.1   *32.2*

Using only triangles, how many interesting shapes can you draw? *(See figures 32.2 through 32.5 for ideas.)* Notice the **implied** triangle in *figure 32.3*. When a triangle is used in a pyramid, what are all of the ways it looks? How does it "feel"? (Big, strong, powerful, heavy, old, immovable, etc.)

32.3   *32.4*   *32.5*

M

When resting on only one of its sides, the triangle is extremely stable, but when tipped onto one of its verticals, it may be either balanced or unstable and may fall over onto one of its sides *(fig. 32.6)*.

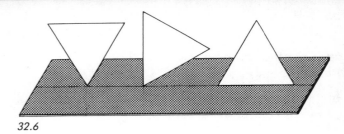

32.6

When one side of a triangle has pressure on it *(fig. 32.7)*, it can't give in without causing the other two sides to give in. This is why it is such a **strong** shape.

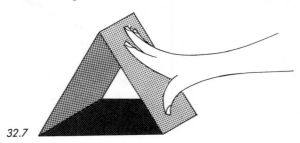

32.7

You can make a triangle by gluing toothpicks, cardboard, balsa wood, or popsicle sticks together . . . and test its strength. This is why architects and builders like triangles so much. Does *your* home have any triangles? Where? Architects may line up several triangles and build a big but very lightweight beam. This is called a **truss.** How many triangles are in the truss in *figure 32.8*? (14) A truss can hold up a roof or a floor.

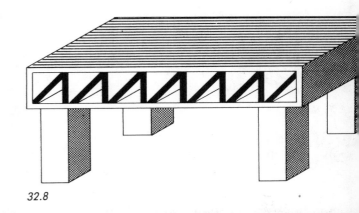

32.8

SUGGESTED ACTIVITIES

You can make a truss with cardboard, balsa wood, or popsicle sticks.

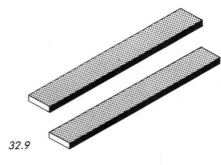

32.9

To make your truss, cut two long strips the same length *(fig. 32.9)*. Now cut several smaller pieces, all the same length *(fig. 32.10)*.

32.10

That's all there is to it. Using glue, make your first triangle on one of the long strips *(fig. 32.11)*. Notice that the first small strip has to stand straight up (perpendicular).

Make another triangle *(fig. 32.12)*, with the first small piece standing straight up, then just keep going to the end.

Now glue the other long side to your triangles *(fig. 32.13)*. Congratulations, you have just made your own truss!

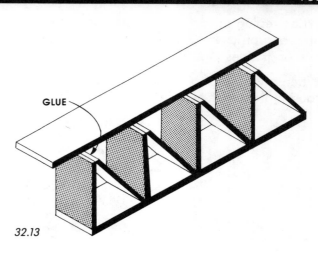

32.13

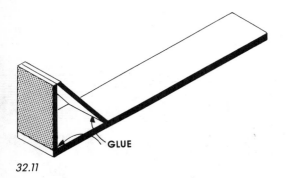

32.11

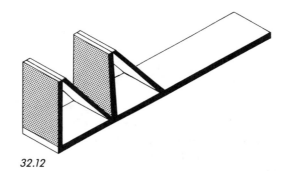

32.12

You can make a **pyramid.** Make four triangles around a square *(fig. 32.14)*. (It helps to leave tabs.) Any stiff paper or cardboard will do.

Now carefully fold the triangles up along the edges of the square, as in *figure 32.15*. You have now made a pyramid! Put glue on the tabs and seal the pyramid shut *(fig. 32.16)*.

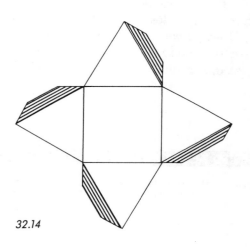

32.14

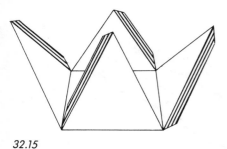

32.15

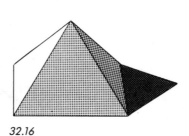

32.16

If you make two pyramids, you can join their square bases to make an octahedron *(fig. 32.17)*.

32.17

Now you can make a 20-sided figure with triangles. *Figure 32.18* shows how.

Join your pyramids, octahedrons, and polyhedron in many beautiful ways.

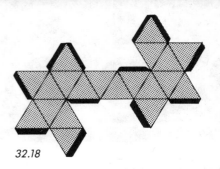

32.18

ALTERNATE ACTIVITIES

1. Use your body to make triangles. *(See figures 32.19 through 32.21 for examples.)*

2. Build some beautiful triangular sculptures (stabiles) using toothpicks, etc.

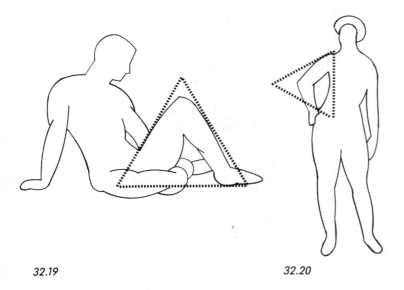

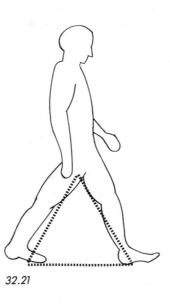

32.19

32.20

32.21

5/33

CONCEPT

Forms and spaces are either positive or negative.

LESSON

As with the lesson on convex and concave forms, we find that any form begins to control space around and within it. The most simple way to explain **negative space** is to say it is "background" to a **positive form.** For example, in the vase exercise *(fig. 33.1)* so popular in the past several decades, we may see the profile faces as positive and the vase as negative. We may see just the opposite.

33.1.

In the old "fly" example *(figs. 33.2 and 33.3),* many people will see only geometric shapes (triangles, squares, etc.) and the word **fly** becomes negative, therefore escaping perception.

33.2.

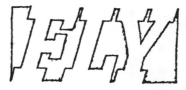

33.3.

F

The Japanese have a word for this positive and negative relationship. It is **notan** (no-TAWN), or the dark/light principle. One popular exercise to teach this perception is that of starting with a square of construction paper and a white backing paper. Next, identical shapes are cut out from each side, flipped over, and glued to the white paper *(fig. 33.4)*. This process is continued, exploring the ''holes'' and their shapes.

Maurice Escher, a Dutch artist, discovered that it is possible to have positive and negative forms interact so that they switch positive and negative identities back and forth easily. In *figure 33.5*, the white horsemen and black horsemen ride in opposite directions, but which is positive space and which is background?

Architects realize that both positive and negative spaces are important. The most obvious example of negative space in architecture is the **air** in a room or a building. Like liquid in a cup, it is defined by the walls, roof, and slabs of a structure. The air spaces are like background.

In *figure 33.6*, the negative spaces come in two ways. One is the sky/air shape as background and environment for the building. The other way is by the spaces below the roof line and, on the ground level, the spaces around the beams and wall masses of the entry.

Figure 33.7 is another example of the use of negative space, by Le Corbusier. The concave roof begins to shape the sky and the spaces between the wall slabs which hold up the roof form. In those slabs, holes (negative spaces) have been ''punched through'' the concrete.

Figure 33.8 is another building by Le Corbusier. Can you see that the negative spaces are defined by the roof slab and its columns? The entry also has negative spaces. As usual, the sky background defines constantly-changing negative spaces as one moves about the building.

33.4.

33.5.

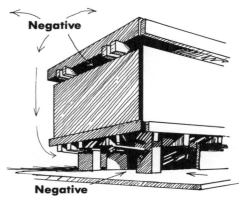

33.8.

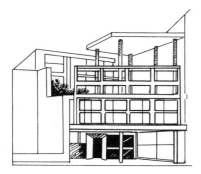

33.6.
Currutchet house, La Plata, Argentina; Le Corbusier, 1949.

33.7.
Legislative Assembly Building, Chandigarh Capitol Complex, India; Le Corbusier, 1961-1964.

List all of the **positive** forms you can think of. (Any object, any tangible thing.) List all of the **negative** spaces. (Holes, air, what objects such as bottles "contain," rooms, halls, gyms, etc.)

Is furniture positive, or negative?

As we walk through a building, the space we walk through is negative. The positive shapes are capable of casting **shadows.** Negative spaces allow **light** to pass through.

Analogy: Positive shapes are to negative space as _____ is to _____.

(Material, air; shadow, light; shape, background.)

In this room (chapel) by Le Corbusier *(fig. 33.9),* the skylights read as either positive or negative. What about the altars, steps, and walls?

33.9.

Cognitive: *Figure 33.10* is a structure of blocks. Identify the positive and negative spaces. Is air the only background for negative space? (No, other slabs of the building may be negative, as in *figure 33.11*.)

33.10.

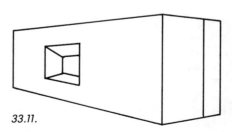

33.11.

Divergent: Create a structure of wood, blocks, rocks, clay, cloth, string, or cardboard, which has interesting and unusual negative spaces. (*Figure 33.12* is an example of a tentlike structure with unusual positive and negative shapes.)

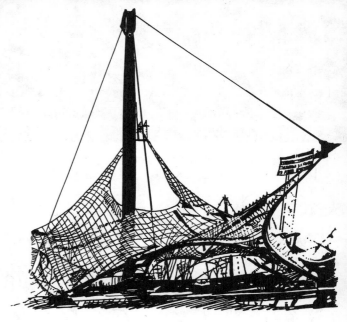

33.12.
Olympic Stadium model, Munich, Germany; Frei Otto, 1971.

Cut out a notan design from dark construction paper and glue cut portions to the white background *(fig. 33.13)*.

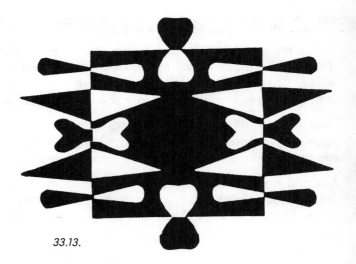

33.13.

5/34

The mass of an architectural design is the geometric bulk or the "look" of the structure. Mass generally influences overall appearance more than any single thing.

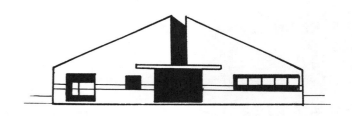

When historians identify the Romanesque Period (1000-1150) in architecture, they describe the buildings as **massive** or geometrically **blocky.** *Figure 34.1* is St. Michael's in Hildesheim in Germany. Do you sense a geometric massing of cones, pyramids, cubes, and rectangles? These are the basic **masses** of the design.

Humans move through architectural space. These usable, interior negative volumes appear as masses (positive forms) when seen as the **exterior.** All architectural designs are compositions of one or more basic related masses.

Massing is a principle based upon the sculptural quality of architecture. The building materials are formed into walls, floors, and roofs. The **voids** are negative space, usually in the form of windows, doors, openings, and spaces around the masses. A good architect develops masterful, exciting, aesthetic relationships between masses and voids.

34.1.
Abbey Church of St. Michael, Hildesheim, Germany; 1001-1031.

C

When designing a building, it must be remembered that each large basic mass consists of smaller parts, such as floors, walls, ceilings, and roofs *(fig. 34.2)*. The contemporary architect may make the **secondary masses** very subtle and subservient to the larger, overall **primary mass** *(fig. 34.3)*.

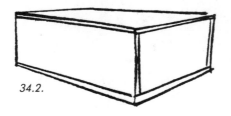

34.2.

34.3.

Some buildings express only the large primary mass of a structure. Usually brick or stone buildings are this type of expression *(fig. 34.4)*. If voids are minimal and masses dominant, the structure will tend to emphasize primary mass.

The well-designed structure has a harmonious balance of masses, and balance between the parts and the whole. Usually, the simple massing of major parts is echoed or reflected in the minor masses or even the voids *(fig. 34.5)*.

34.5.

34.4.

Sometimes the **structure** of the building is expressed as a **secondary design mass.** These structural masses may be large beams or concrete slabs *(fig. 34.6)*.

34.6.

When a child plays with building blocks, he or she is dealing with basic masses *(fig. 34.7).* Recall that Frank Lloyd Wright said the best and most basic architectural training he ever had was at his mother's knee, playing with Froebel blocks.

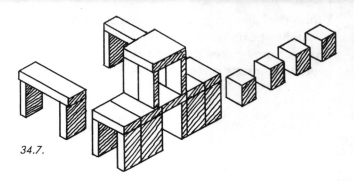

34.7.

The **basic mass** concept is very prevalent in the New Brutalism style of architecture which "honestly" expresses structure and material without covering them up or concealing them. In *figure 34.8* we see the basic concrete/masonry box slab used with beams, columns, and walls in a no-nonsense expression.

34.8.

The difference between a mass and a void is almost identical to that between positive and negative form and space. The only difference is that a void may sometimes be part of the primary mass, as with the glass box expressions *(figs. 34.9 and 34.10),* where windows are voids, determining the configuration of the mass. Understanding this, complete this analogy:

Mass is to void as _____ is to _____.

Looking about the room, what are all of the voids you see? All of the masses?

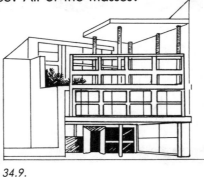

34.9.   34.10.

Cognitive: Trace a picture of a building from a magazine and label all of the masses, as in *figure 34.11.*

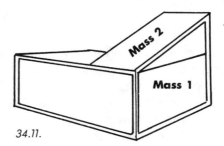

34.11.

Divergent: Design a building form which gives more attention to voids than masses. *(Figure 34.12 is an example.)*

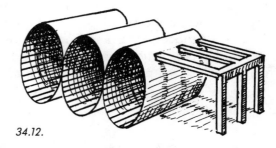

34.12.

5/35

Spaces may be organized either symmetrically, asymmetrically, or radially.

What does it mean to have **balance?** Balance is when opposing forces or weights are equal. (They are in a state of equilibrium.) The best example from life experience is a teeter-totter *(fig. 35.1)*. The only way a smaller person can offset a larger one is to be on a longer portion of board.

This is also true in architecture. When the smaller portion is further away from center, it can balance a larger or heavier portion. In art this is known as **informal** or **unequal balance.** If something is identical on both or all sides of the center, it has a **formal balance** *(fig. 35.2)*. Sometimes architects call formal balance **symmetrical.** They call informal balance **asymmetrical** *(fig. 35.3)*. Sometimes things are balanced all about a center, and that is called **radial balance** *(fig. 35.4)*.

Sometimes a building is formal because it uses **classical** proportions, details, or materials. For instance, if the building has an entry with perfectly-fitted polished marble, finely finished wall surfaces, and a symmetrical design, it will probably be **formal.** On the other hand, if it uses rough-sawn cedar, irregularly-spaced rock walls, and an asymmetrical layout, it will probably be **informal.**

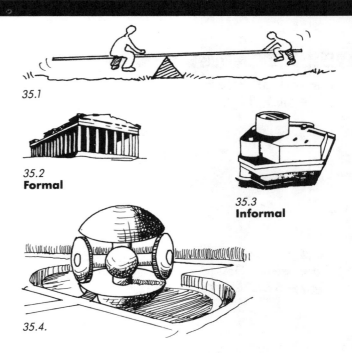

35.1

35.2
Formal

35.3
Informal

35.4.

C

When we deal with asymmetry or symmetry relative to balance, it is interesting that balance can be achieved by adjusting weight and location, by focusing attention, and by contrasts. Symmetry gives a sense of stability to a design. Even when an arrangement is just "psychologically" balanced, it *seems* symmetrical.

Figures 35.5 through 35.13 are buildings which tend to be either more symmetric or more asymmetric. Can you tell which they are?

35.5.
Notice that this house by Bernard Maybeck has the main wing with the gable symmetrical, yet the overall composition is informal, or asymmetrical.

35.6.
Legislative Assembly Building, Chandigarh Capitol Complex, India; Le Corbusier, 1961-1964.

35.8.
Colosseum Amphiteater, Rome, Italy; A.D. **70-82.**

35.9.
The Guggenheim Museum, New York; Frank Lloyd Wright, 1943-1959.

35.7.
Qian Mien, Peking, China; periodically rebuilt through the centuries.

35.10.
This dome by Buckminster Fuller is radially balanced.

35.11.
Stepped Pyramid, Egypt; c. 2750 B.C.

35.12.
Transamerica Building, San Francisco; William Pereira Associates, 1972.

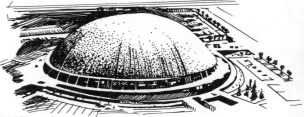

35.13.
This sports arena in Italy is radially balanced.

Few buildings are as formal as the Greek and Roman classical temples *(fig. 35.14)*.

The Japanese architects were masters of asymmetrical design *(fig. 35.15)*.

35.14.

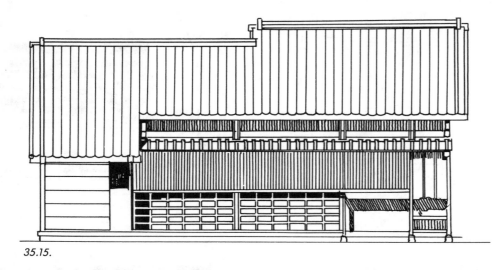

35.15.

PRODUCTIVE THINKING

Find a radially balanced object, an asymmetrical object, and a symmetrical object.

Take some balanced poses in front of a mirror *(fig. 35.16)*. Identify the axis (center) of the pose.

Simile: The building was as formal as _____. (A black tuxedo, a spinning top.)

The structure was so asymmetrical it looked like _____. (A lever under a rock; a tipping, whirling saucer.)

35.16.

Cognitive: Draw a formal (symmetrical) house *(fig. 35.17)*. Draw an informal (asymmetrical) house *(fig. 35.18)*.

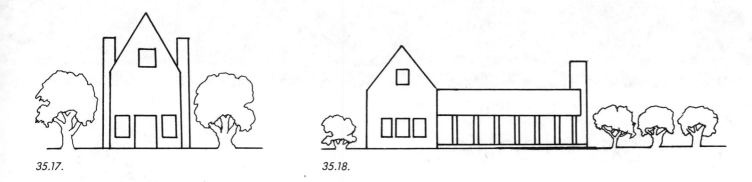

35.17.   35.18.

Divergent: Create a radially balanced, asymmetrical structure *(figs. 35.19 and 35.20)*.

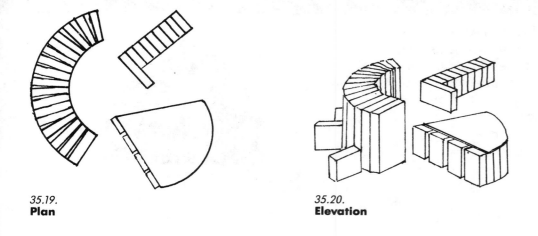

35.19.   35.20.
Plan   **Elevation**

ALTERNATE ACTIVITIES

Take a walk to find formal and informal buildings, gardens, or objects.

Why are civic buildings, such as capitols, usually quite formal looking?

5/36

Roof systems have a particular "look" and may be identified easily.

One of the most basic of human needs is shelter. The world of architecture arose to meet that need. The **roof** is the most immediate, primitive way to shelter something. In Samoa, Fiji, or Tahiti, a roof is all that is really needed because the climate is warm year round. Architectural structures on those islands are very "roof oriented," to protect from rain *(fig. 36.1)*. Walls are not for temperature control, but for a bit of privacy. There are also social and religious reasons for such **open** design.

Following is a chart of the basic roof forms:

36.1.

ROOF

36.2. Gable

36.4. Flat or "Built-up"

36.6. Mansard

THE STYLE IN USE

36.3.

36.5.

36.7.

FUNCTION

36.2-36.3. Quick run-off of rain and snow.

Visually dynamic.

Strong triangular form (rigid).

36.4-36.5. Easy to build—uses few materials.

Straight lines (horizontal emphasis).

Tar paper, tar, and gravel built up.

36.6-36.7. A French variation on the basic gable—for style and decorative quality. (A flat portion at the very top.)

ROOF

36.8. **Hipped (Hip)**

36.10. **Double Hip (and variations)**

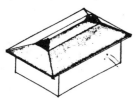

36.12. **Shed**

THE STYLE IN USE

36.9.

36.11.

36.13.

FUNCTION

36.8-36.11. Emphasizes horizontality.

Drains well on all sides.

Handles deep overhanging eaves well.

36.12-36.13. Excellent solar energy collector.

Is ''half a gable,'' therefore provides excellent drainage but more possibilities for ''head room'' and light.

Another version is the ''salt box'' style.

Easy to build.

ROOF

36.14. Butterfly

36.16. Gambrel (Dutch) (English)

36.18. Monitor

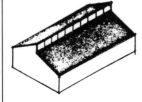

THE STYLE IN USE

36.15.

36.17.

36.19.

FUNCTION

36.14-36.15. An inverted gable.

May have drainage problems if slopes not perfectly handled.

Allows two shed roofs to be joined, giving maximum light intake.

36.16-36.17. A flattened gable, then steep, then flat angled again (bell-like).

36.18-36.19. Drains well.

Allows second story.

Provides porch roof by extension of eaves.

ROOF

36.20. Flying Gable

36.22. Sculptural Varieties (including domes, etc.)

36.24. Jerkin or "Clipped Gable"

THE STYLE IN USE

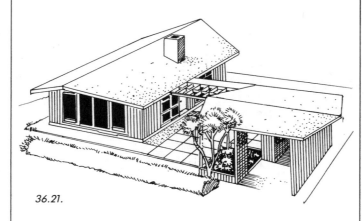

36.21.

36.23.

36.25.

FUNCTION

36.20-36.21. Drains well.

Allows additional light intake from highest point.

Allows for a loft or partial second story.

Drains well.

Extends to deep eaves on the ends.

Shades end walls.

36.22-36.23. Functional needs create space for that use; the molding of space is sculptural.

36.24-36.25. "Softens" a gable.

Good drainage.

Relates to other design requirements.

Cognitive: Identify the roof styles in *figures 36.26 through 36.29.*

36.26.
Answer _____

36.27.
Answer _____

36.28.
Answer _____

36.29.
Answer _____

SUGGESTED ACTIVITIES

Take a neighborhood "identity walk." Find as many roof styles as possible.

6/37

All architectural structure is geometric, whether organic or mechanical.

LESSON

Whenever a positive form is constructed, space is enclosed or defined. In order to build something which is strong and safe for shelter, the architect must understand forces, weight, strength of materials, action and reaction, and visual appeal.

As we learned in Lesson 5/33, triangles are one of our most stable geometric forms. They are the basis of the **truss** *(fig. 37.1)*. The truss is used to span large spaces and so requires great strength. The truss parts are made so that they act together as a large **beam,** though much lighter in weight than a solid beam. Generally the parts of the truss are triangular shapes or connections.

37.1.

If you gently bend a plastic stick or a twig *(fig. 37.2)*, then take away your strength or force that bent it, what does it do? It returns to its original shape. This is called **reaction.** Your arms causing it to bend by force are **action.** Action **changes** its condition of rest or motion or form.

37.2.

Forces (such as your arms causing the bending) have three parts or measures: **magnitude, direction, and position.**

B

That's about all you need to know to understand how architectural structure works. For example, the **beam** is the most simple structure. It may be made of any material strong enough to hold up under pressure. The top of the beam, where the boy is causing a downward force with his weight *(fig. 37.3)*, is in **compression** (trying to get shorter). The bottom of the beam is in **tension** (trying to get longer). Press down on the tip of your finger with your other hand's thumb. This is compression. Pull on your finger; this is tension. Elastics are wonderful in tension—but what about compression?

37.3.

A truss does the same thing as a beam *(fig. 37.4)*, but it is **lighter** because it is not solid wood, or solid concrete, etc. It is made of smaller parts, fitted together as triangles.

37.4.

Stone and brick have been used for centuries for buildings because they are so good in **compression.** (You can pile or stack them and they hold up weight very well.) But stone and brick aren't very good in tension—not much stretching strength. They are better as walls than ceilings *(fig. 37.5)*, because ceilings have to span large distances. Early architects, called "master-builders," did use stone for ceilings, but they had to figure out how to have ceilings in compression, like walls. They found the **arch.** The arch used forces from a **keystone**—again a triangle shape—to press down and out on all of the other stones *(fig. 37.6)*. Gothic cathedrals employed the most creative use of stone as ceiling. It was called the arch-vault (or a series of arches).

37.5.

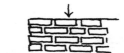

Today steel, concrete, and plastics allow us to enjoy much lighter roof systems. As a result, we can have virtually any shape roof we want over virtually any shape room space we want.

Keystone.

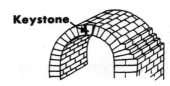

37.6.

Using toothpicks, straws, or commercial products like D-Stix[1] you can explore the new forms which are possible. If you like symmetrical forms, you might be interested to know that there are only five "regular" (symmetrical) polyhedrons (many-sided figures):

1. Tetrahedron *(fig. 37.7)* (the triangle-base pyramid).

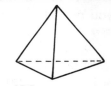

37.7.
Tetrahedron

2. Hexahedron *(fig. 37.8)* (the cube).

3. Octahedron *(fig. 37.9)* (two pentahedrons).

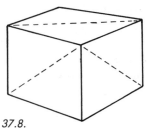

37.8.
Hexahedron

4. Dodecahedron *(fig. 37.10)* (made of pentagons).

37.9.
Octahedron

37.10
Dodecahedron

5. Isosahedron *(fig. 37.11)* (20 triangles).

37.11.
Isosahedron

1. D-Stix may be purchased from: D-Stix, Division of Geodestix, P. O. Box 11893, Spokane, WA 99211.

PRODUCTIVE THINKING

What are all of the symmetrical forms you can think of? (Apples, boxes, stars, starfish, flowers, pine cones, prisms, crystals, etc.)

Analogy: Stone is to compression as elastic is to _____. (Tension.)

Elastic is to compression as stone is to _____. (Tension.)

Cognitive: Construct a tetrahedron, using straws and clay, glue and clay with toothpicks, or D-Stix.

Construct a pentahedron. Construct a dodecahedron.

Divergent: Using orderly lengths of material (straws, toothpicks, stix, etc.), create a tower or space center *(fig. 37.12 is an example).* Make it unique and unlike anything you've seen before.

Consider the simplicity, order, unity, and beauty of geometric forms.

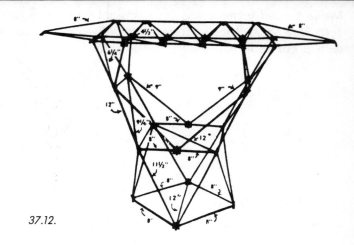

37.12.

Visit power line tower structures *(37.13 and 37.14).* Can you recreate their designs with other materials?

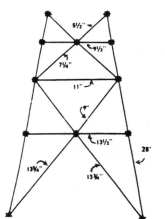

37.13.

Look through a microscope at crystal forms.

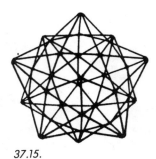

37.15.

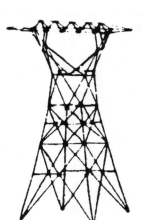

37.14.

Make curved forms using only straight lines. In *figures 37.16 and 37.17,* simply connect 1 to 1, 2 to 2, 3 to 3, and so on. When all numbers are connected you will see a form with a **curve** in it.

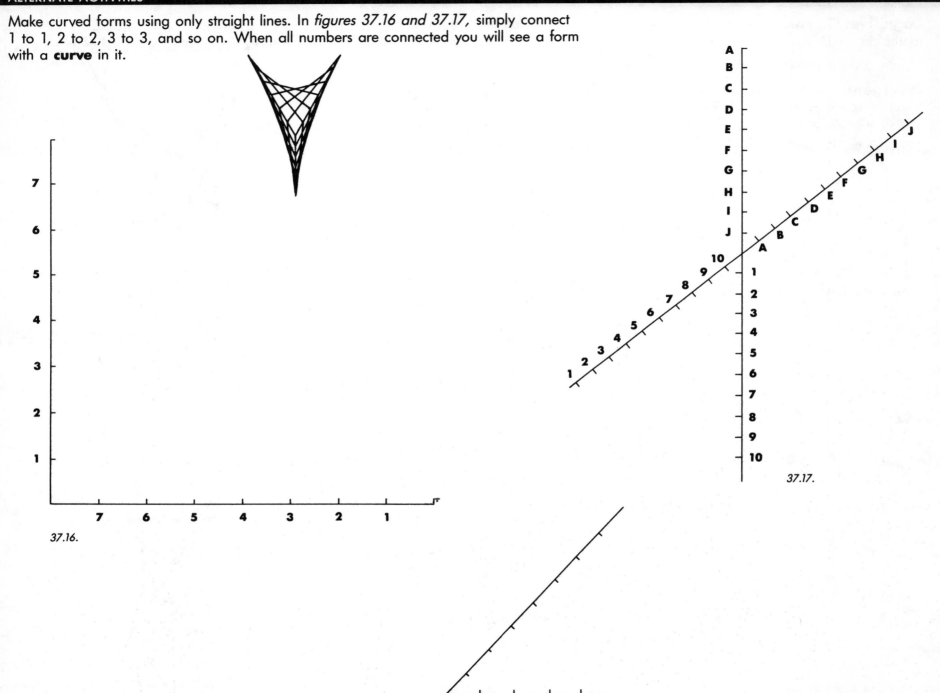

37.16.

37.17.

37.18.

CONCEPT

Almost all visual stimuli present a pattern, but sometimes pattern may be difficult to perceive.

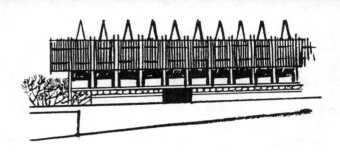

LESSON

Pattern seeking is the first step in all perception.

As we saw in Lesson 2/10, pattern is created whenever lines, shapes, forms, colors, and values are repeated. While this is quite simple and easy to understand, many designers fail to perceive pattern. In the logo above, can you see that pattern is the dominant part of that composition?

As we studied **massing** in architectural design, it became apparent that major masses create a pattern, but pattern may also give the surface of a mass more interest. (Most textures are also patterns.)

Can you see how the building in *figure 38.1* has a pattern which is almost like the plaid of a tartan?

In this pattern by Vaserely *(fig. 38.2),* the illusion of a warped surface is created by distortion of the repeated squares. It is obviously the same pattern, but with purposeful distortion.

38.1.

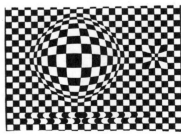

38.2.

c

In these computerized patterns, it becomes very difficult to perceive a pattern which is *within* another pattern. For example, *figure 38.3* is a pattern of the letter **R**. There is a smaller square within the big primary square of **R**'s. Do you see it? (Solution is in *figure 38.4*. The hidden pattern is created by all backward **R**'s.)

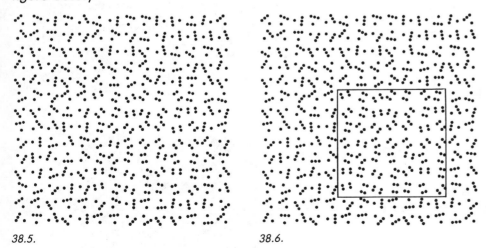

38.3.   38.4.

Try another hidden pattern. Find the hidden square in *figure 38.5*. (The answer is in *figure 38.6*.)

38.5.   38.6.

Figure 38.7 shows one more hidden pattern. Do you see the smaller square of pattern in this one?

Simile: A hidden pattern is like a _____. Can you think of a way the army uses this concept? (For camouflage, codes, anything secretive.)

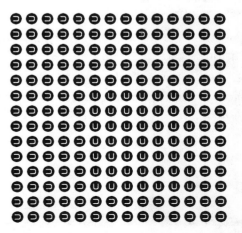

38.7.

Cognitive and Divergent: Our eyes have a natural pattern-seeking tendency. Look at the pattern in *figure 38.8.* It is made up entirely of straight lines and squares, *in* a square. But in spite of all the straight lines, what do you see? What happens when you try to trace one of the ephemeral swirls?

Most artists and architects "rough in" an overall gestalt or pattern before drawing in detail. (Gestalt means "order" or "organizational essence.")

Use finger paints to create a pattern using fingers, knuckles, combs, or objects. Simply **repeat** something you do in the paint, over and over again. (Poster paint, water, flour, and water-soluble paste make an easy batch of finger paint.)

Next, design a building with a wall which could use your new pattern, as in *figure 38.9.*

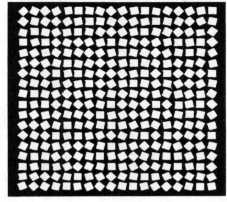

38.8.

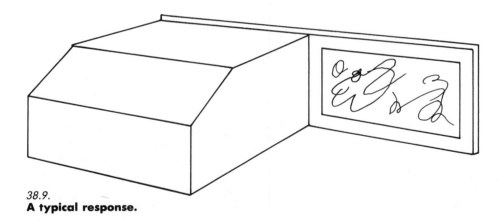

38.9.
A typical response.

Architects often use light and shadow to create a secondary pattern of their mass patterns. Take an excursion to find shadow patterns. *Figures 38.10 through 38.13* show some architectural uses of light and shadow pattern.

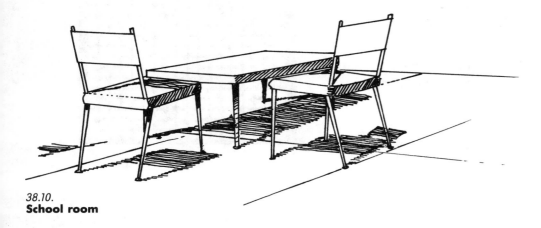

38.10.
School room

38.11.
Trees

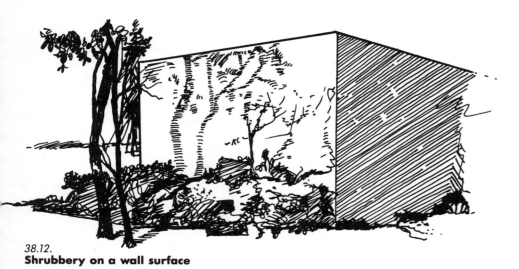

38.12.
Shrubbery on a wall surface

38.13.
On an architectural structure

LEVEL 7 ACTIVITY
6/39

A balancing of complexity (detail) and simplicity (plainness) is necessary in architecture.

One problem the lay citizen and contractor (builder) sometimes have is that they try to put everything they have ever seen into their home or building, as in *figure 39.1.* They want bricks with rock, and wood with wrought iron railings, columns, glass, and steel frames. When they finish, they display a "museum" of everything they could gather up. The result is chaotic and busy, with no visual relief or order. People need to understand how a skillful designer or architect keeps order and unity by a balance of **complexity** and **simplicity.**

39.1.

The wall plane and the overall structural forms are the two main issues in complexity and simplicity. The texture of a plane's surface, together with its color, determines its apparent visual weight or attention, scale, and attitude. If too many forms are thrown together, the result lacks unity and harmony *(fig. 39.2).* The viewer feels uneasy when looking at too many unrelated elements. In music, it is easy to **hear** this in a perceptual sense. Play two very different tapes or records at the same time. The result will probably be chaotic and almost painful to hear. At best, it will be nerve-racking and distasteful.

39.2.

L

While variety adds interest to a design, too *much* variety may cause visual chaos and pollution. Using anything and everything which comes to mind is generally too much.

On the other hand, a total lack of variety may cause visual boredom *(fig. 39.3).*

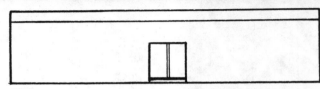

39.3.

When a building uses too many elements we say it is "busy." When a building uses no variety in elements we say it is too plain or uninteresting. The architect must have a balance of **simplicity** and restful visual areas with **complex,** more active forms.

Notice that in *figure 39.4,* a Renaissance palazzo (Palace by Michelozzi), the top floor is finished with less texture in the stones. The third floor is a rest from the textures of the roof cornice and the masonry of the two bottom floors.

39.4.
Palazzo Medici-Riccard, Florence, Italy; Michelozzi, 1444-1460.

In *figure 39.5,* architect Richard Meier gave the home a balance by a variety of angled corners and different ceiling heights. Without these variations the home would have been much too plain or simple.

39.5.
Hoffman house, East Hampton, New York; Richard Meier, 1966.

In the CBS Building by Saarinen *(fig. 39.7),* the architect evidently felt that the only variety necessary was in the "folded" wall surface *(fig. 39.6).*

39.6.

Do *you* think this variation is enough to keep the building an interesting form to look at? (The other structures around it help add visual variety to the wall surface by casting their shadows over the surface at different times of day.)

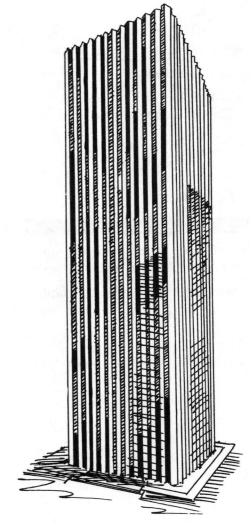

39.7.
CBS Building, New York City; Saarinen and Associates, 1962-1964.

Draw as many "simple" forms as you can. *Figure 39.8* gives some clues.

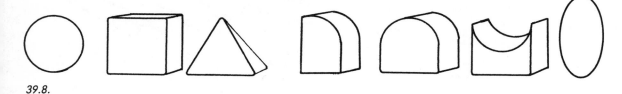

39.8.

Make up a form which is ridiculously complex, as in *figure 39.9*.

Analogy: An orange is to a simple form (sphere) as a _____ is to _____.

(Oil refinery, complexity.)

Simile: A building with no variety is as boring as _____. (T.V. show with video trouble, PBS discussion, a book in a foreign language.)

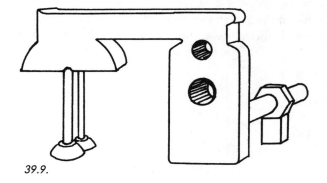

39.9.

Cognitive: Using cutout shapes from construction paper, create a design which is too busy and has virtually no space without shapes and texture in it, as in *figure 39.10*.

Divergent: Create a toothpick sculpture (or straw, popsicle stick, etc.) which has an unusual form but does *not* become too busy.

39.10.

6/40

Shadows are an important visual element in architectural design. Shadows define form, make texture visible, and provide shade and contrast.

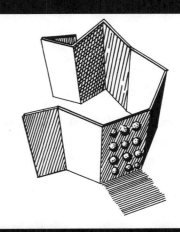

"There is no perception without contrast." —Franklin Y. Gates, Design Engineer

Night is just a giant shadow. As evening shadows get longer and longer, eventually total shadow (or night) occurs. Architects may plan to create night shadow on their buildings using spotlights. They realize that our eyes require light and **shadow** in order to see form.

The sun is our **natural** source of light for the illumination of forms and spaces in buildings. Light and its effect on a structure change with each hour of the day and from season to season and according to the weather.

As the sun changes patterns of light and shade in a structure, it animates those spaces and articulates the forms and textures.

Color is also determined by light. The effects of sunlight may create delightful, playful moods or more melancholy, somber moods.

F

The artist Monét realized the importance of light and shadow in his studies of haystacks and the Rouen Cathedral in various types of light. Gothic details change in mood with each change of light. (See any book about Monét and his work.)

The **texture** of a material, such as brick, is brought out nicely by the play of light and shadow on its surface. Perception of texture is directly related to shadows. This is demonstrated beautifully by the flat pencil sketch in *figure 40.1.*

40.1.

Relief sculpture on a building is seen readily because of shadow. The sculpture changes its appearance during each hour of the day *(fig. 40.2).*

40.2.
Relief frieze on Arca Pacis Augustae, Rome; 13 B.C.

PRODUCTIVE THINKING

Similes: Because so little contrast is seen, night makes one as blind as a _____.

A building without shadows is like _____.

What are all of the things in or on buildings which shadows help us to see? (Entries, windows, porches, sculpture, etc.)

Notice how shadow helps one to perceive the forms in this house by Gwathmey and Siegel. The curves, indentations, and undersides are perceived through shadow configurations *(fig. 40.3).*

40.3.
Gwathmey house, Amagansett, New York; Charles Gwathmey and Gwathmey Siegel, 1965-1967.

Shadows help us to understand the forms which Le Corbusier has chosen for the cathedral in *figure 40.4* and this governor's mansion *(fig. 40.5)* in India. The overhangs, windows, entries and roof line are dramatically emphasized by shadow.

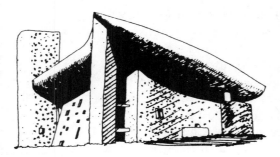

40.4.
Notre Dame du Haut, Ronchamp, France; Le Corbusier, 1950-1955.

40.5.
Governor's Palace, Chandigarh, India; Le Corbusier, c. 1957.

The ancient Egyptians, living in a very warm area, designed their buildings to use many shady, cool interiors with few windows *(fig. 40.6)*. In Rome, entries are articulated by shaded porticoes *(fig. 40.7)*.

40.6.
Entry pylons, Temple of Horus at Edfu, Egypt; 237-257 B.C.

40.7.
The Pantheon, Rome; A.D. 118-125.

Cognitive and Divergent: In today's technological world, an aesthetic sensitivity to personalities and characteristics of materials tends to atrophy. This exercise will help build your understanding as you design one small textured element which is largely dependent on light and shadow.

1. Fold a piece of paper into fourths *(fig. 40.8)*.

2. Use a variety of "tools" to put a different texture into each quadrant *(fig. 40.9)*. For example, a sharp pencil, ice pick, stretched-out paper clip, pin of a compass, or a straight pin may be used to carefully poke textural holes into one quadrant. Another approach might be to gently moisten one quadrant and, just before it is totally dry, press a metal punch, empty ballpoint pen casing, or any stylus onto the damp surface. Exacto knives (though they must be used carefully) can be used to cut shapes into the surface, and the tabs may be folded as well. The head of a nail may be gently hammered, with heavy and light strokes, onto the surface. Chisels create interesting textures, and some textures may even be embossed by a rubbing process.

3. Use different light sources to see how changing light and shadow affect the texture. The texture you have created could be made of plaster, plastic, or concrete on a wall surface.

Another version of such a textural/relief exercise can be done by rolling out slabs of clay, and then using various tools to imprint a texture into the clay surface. (See *Art Is Elementary* Lessons 43 and 107.)

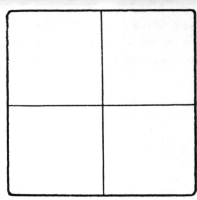

40.8.

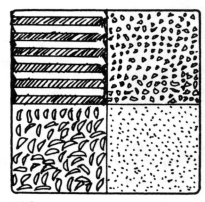

40.9.

Try to find buildings with unusual relief textures on their walls. *Figures 40.10-40.13* are some examples.

With a portable light source, study the effect light has on faces, objects, and sculpture.

Make a texture sample using wood scraps, moldings, stones, etc. Then place the sample under a light source and discover the various effects.

40.10.

40.11

40.12

40.13.

CONCEPT

A point is the basic unit in art. When extended, a point becomes a line, a line becomes a plane, a plane becomes a form with volume.

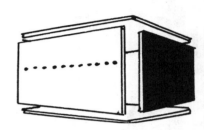

LESSON

Most architects use lines, shapes, and forms to plan their buildings. Lines can make shapes, and shapes can make forms. (This Euclidean model for design is today being challenged by some who feel that this "box" concept is limited and unnatural. They feel that the forms of nature are a more human, more creative model for design.) *Figure 41.1* is a **point** or a dot. It is just a little mark.

If we "push" or extend the dot or point *(fig. 41.2)*, it can make a **line.** Two points describe a line which connects them.

Architects use lines to indicate walls, fences, and shapes *(figs. 41.3 and 41.4)*. They use the idea of "implied line."

41.1.

41.2.

41.3.

41.4.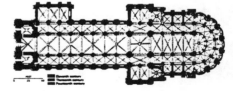

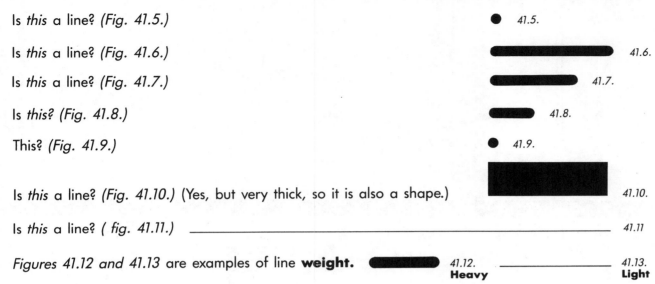

Is *this* a line? *(Fig. 41.5.)*   ● 41.5.

Is *this* a line? *(Fig. 41.6.)*   41.6.

Is *this* a line? *(Fig. 41.7.)*   41.7.

Is *this?* *(Fig. 41.8.)*   41.8.

This? *(Fig. 41.9.)*   ● 41.9.

Is *this* a line? *(Fig. 41.10.)* (Yes, but very thick, so it is also a shape.)   41.10.

Is *this* a line? *(fig. 41.11.)* _____ 41.11

Figures 41.12 and 41.13 are examples of line **weight.**   41.12.   _____ 41.13.
                                                              Heavy   **Light**

When **edges** meet, we "feel" a line. Find an example of an edge line in your room.

If we could drag this line along *(fig. 41.14),* it would extend itself into a shape or a **plane.**

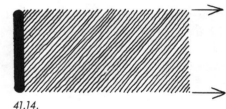

41.14.

Put a straight line of finger paints, colored chalk, or pastels on a surface. Now use a piece of cardboard (or a flat-edged ruler) to "extend" the line, as in *figure 41.15.* It will make a **shape** or a plane. (You can use silk-screen squeegees for this, or even windshield scrapers.) If you make a line with several colors of paint, your plane will be like a rainbow shape.

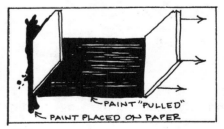

PAINT "PULLED"
PAINT PLACED ON PAPER
41.15.

Most walls in buildings are planes. Posts make it **seem** as if a plane or wall is there *(fig. 41.16).*

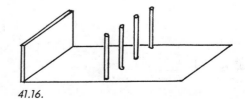

41.16.

Shape is a plane's primary identity. We see the **true** shape of plane only when we look at it directly from the front *(figs. 41.17 through 41.19)*.

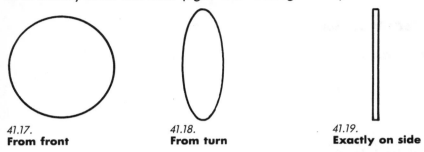

41.17.
From front

41.18.
From turn

41.19.
Exactly on side

PRODUCTIVE THINKING

Shapes are two-dimensional. If you pile up some circles (poker chips or money) they make a _____.

If you pile up a lot of squares, they become a _____.

Planes—serving as walls, ceilings, or floors—may be the boundaries of a **form,** or a volume *(figs. 41.22 through 41.24)*.

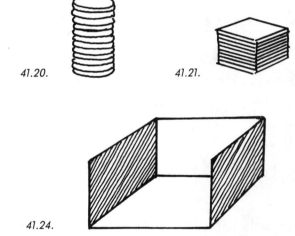

41.20.

41.21.

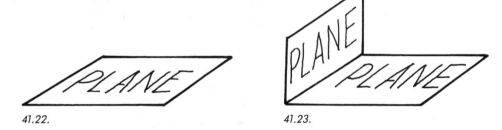

41.22.

41.23.

41.24.

Figures 41.25 and 41.26 show some ways architects use **planes** in their plans.

41.25.

41.26.

How many shapes can you name? What are all of the "circle things"? What are all of the "triangle things"?

Try folding a sheet of paper into a most unusual form *(fig. 41.27)*. (Books on origami may give initial clues for this activity. See also the alternative activities below.)

41.27.

When looking at a form, there are always points, lines, and planes. What are all of the points in *figure 41.28?* Where are the lines? Where are the planes?

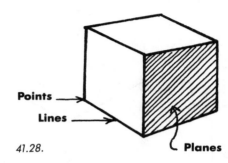

Points ——

Lines ——

41.28.

Planes

SUGGESTED ACTIVITIES

Build a "card castle" or cardboard structure *(fig. 41.29)*. Glue may be used to seal connections of cardboard planes. Explore differences in planes as **ground** or as **floor**. Toothpick structures may be built with glued connections and paper planes.

41.29.

Explore a variety of surfaces of ceiling and wall planes *(fig. 41.30)*.

Could you design a building which would *not* be based on planes?

41.30.

Try folding this form *(fig. 41.31),* using stiff paper, and count the **points, lines,** and **planes.**

Create piled up shapes with cardboard, plastic, etc.*(fig. 41.32).*

Take a walk through your neighborhood and identify points, lines, and planes as you go.

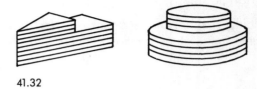

41.32

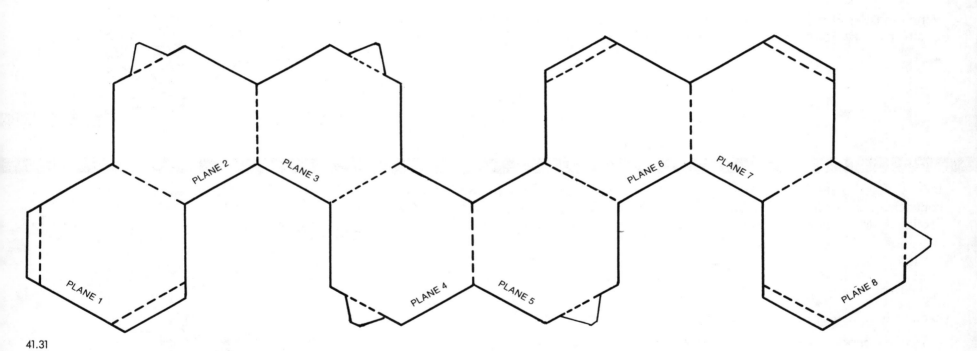

PLANE 1
PLANE 2
PLANE 3
PLANE 4
PLANE 5
PLANE 6
PLANE 7
PLANE 8

41.31

CONCEPT

Objects and forms may be grouped or arranged in ways useful in architectural design.

LESSON

Grouping may emphasize form, color, size, texture, shape, or even function. Grouping (or **clustering,** as it is sometimes called) may occur in **plan** *(fig. 42.1)* or in **elevation** *(fig. 42.2).* It is a principle by which elements are organized by proximity and likeness into pleasing and functional **units.**

Grouped organizations can encompass forms and spaces which are dissimilar but related only by grouping **proximity.** Dissimilar elements may also be grouped about a point, an axis, or a "traffic pattern" or flow through the architecture. Grouped organizations readily tolerate growth and change due to their **flexibility.** In a grouped organization, since it is "the group" which is emphasized, dominance is only achieved by size, form, orientation, or color, and so on *(fig. 42.3).* Romanesque architects (1000-1150) designed cathedrals which were grouped around a monasterial function with basic geometrical forms.

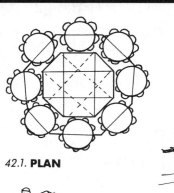

42.1. PLAN

42.2.
ELEVATION

42.3.
View of Cluny, France; c. 1085.

G

The tower roofs were conical or pyramidal *(fig. 42.4.)*, the apse or altar end cylindrical and domed, and the rest a series of cubes and rectangles—all grouped into one large, unified whole.

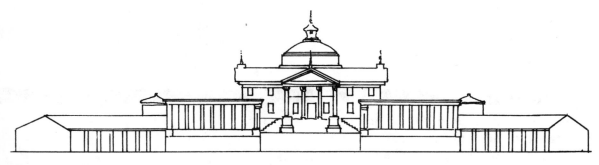

As the Renaissance drew to a close, the Mannerist Period followed with work like that in *figure 42.5* by Palladio in Italy, which is grouped formally or symmetrically about the classical center rotunda.

42.4.

42.5.
Villa Trissino in Meledo, Italy; Andrea Palladio, c. 1550.

In the twentieth century, architects still use grouping as a design tool. The Opera House in Sydney, Australia *(fig. 42.6)*, by Jorn Utzon, has natural shell forms grouped into a rhythmic unit. They are grouped by proximity, similar form, color, and texture of material.

42.6.
Sydney Opera House, Australia; Jorn Utzon, 1959-1973.

Name all of the things you can think of which come in groups or clusters. (Grapes, pebbles, vegetables, people, branches and twigs, grass clumps, etc.)

What doesn't belong in this group *(fig. 42.7)?*

Analogy: A herd is to sheep as a _____ is to _____.

(Covey, quail; crowd, people.)

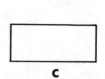

42.7.   **A**   **B**   **C**   **D**   **E**

Use two colors of construction paper to cut out some triangle shapes, rectangle shapes, and circle shapes.

Cognitive: Using four or five of your rectangle shapes, group them into two clusters, by **proximity** *(fig. 42.8).*

42.8.

Group all your circle shapes into two clusters by **similarity** *(fig. 42.9).* (Notice that the shapes in a haphazard configuration may be as interesting as the arranged ones.)

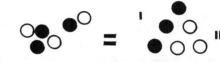

42.9.

Group *all* of your shapes into one cluster by **line of direction** or **path** *(fig. 42.10).*

42.10.

Divergent: Choose a basic architectural form, such as a cylinder, triangle, etc. Now make a composition with several of that form and one other form of your choice. The composition must develop a unified structure by grouping those basic forms, as in *figure 42.11.*

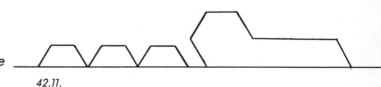

42.11.

Consider the Romanesque-Gothic design principle of grouping according to a monasterial need, such as safety, independence, farming, religion, turbulent times, knights, crusades, etc.

CONCEPT

Architects use color in a variety of ways. The value of a color is affected by the values around it.

LESSON

The most obvious use of color by architects today is in **super graphics.** Architects combine bright color with linear forms and arrowlike "direction indicators" to **get attention** and **direct movement.** The graphics are usually on walls, but may even be on floors and ceilings, as in factories and hospitals. In *figure 43.1,* a bicyclist follows super graphics on the road and, in Japan, a building by Takeyama *(fig. 43.2)* exhibits gigantic super graphics.

43.1.

43.2.

F

Figure 43.3 is a generally uninteresting building wall which is now very dynamic by virtue of super graphics.

Architects may lead people about a building by having them follow one color line until they find their particular destination.

Another important use of color is to **harmonize** with environment. In a beautiful European town *(fig. 43.4)*, made of gray or brown stone buildings, a brightly colored plastic building may look too harsh. It shouts and screams for attention like a spoiled child.

All colors, however, will harmonize with black, white, and gray. All colors have a **value,** or darkness. If you take a black and white photograph of colored objects, you can see their relative darknesses and lightnesses in value.

Traditional school buildings are often the most violated buildings in our environment for color relationships. Architects have a name for such drab, uninteresting colors—''institutional colors''—and these range from pale green to dull beige and yellowish off-whites.

Some of the most interesting architectural innovations in color were the stained glass windows in the Gothic style (1100-1400). Rose windows were giant, colorful focal points representing the all-seeing eye of God and the wheel of fortune in life. English architects took such stained-glass art to its ultimate expression during the ''Perpendicular Period'' of their Gothic style (from 1377 to 1500), with large expanses of glass *(fig. 43.5)*.

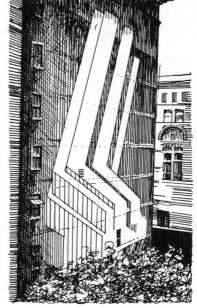

43.3.

43.4.
Castle Combe, England.

43.5
Amiens Cathedral, Amien, France; 1220-1236.

After the Gothic style and Renaissance Classicism, the Baroque Period left the "dark" atmosphere of stained-glass illumination and sought white interiors lighted by **clear** glass. Color was achieved by beautiful murals and paintings on the brightly-lit interiors.

One of the most forward-looking uses of color in architecture is found in the Pompidou Center in Paris, by Piano and Rogers (1977) *(fig. 43.6).*

43.6.
**Pompidou Center, Paris;
Piano and Rogers, 1977.**

PRODUCTIVE THINKING

What color should a photographer's dark room be? (Black.) Why?

What color should a hospital operating room be? Why?

What color would you like your room to be? Why?

What is your favorite fruit? Do you like that color?

Which colors are **warm** feeling? Which colors seem **cool?** Do you associate other feelings with color?

Simile: A blue apple is like a _____.

Analogy: An ice cream store painted black is to customers as _____ is to _____.

Colors are to buildings as _____ is to _____.

SUGGESTED ACTIVITIES

Convergent: If you wanted a building to appear quiet, i.e., in the background and non-obtrusive, what are the colors you might choose?

If you wanted a building to boldly come forward and be noticed, what color would you use?

What are super graphics?

Divergent: Design a super graphic for your room or hallway at home *(fig. 43.7).* Use an 8½"×11" sheet of paper. Use harmonious or complementary colors with dark borders. Work your name or logo into the design, if you wish.

Find examples of excellent color decisions in your community.

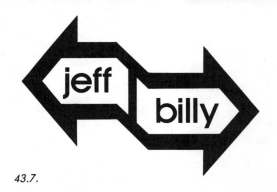

43.7.

LEVEL / ACTIVITY
7/44

CONCEPT

Architects may plan entire cities.

LESSON

Not only do architects design buildings, but occasionally they are fortunate enough to be asked to plan an entire city or a large part of that city. **City planning** or **urban design** is a large business today *(fig. 44.1)*.

When a government is making major civic growth plans, it may be necessary to "start fresh" with a new city in a new location. Such an example is Brasilia, in the center of Brazil. The logo above shows some of the buildings in this twentieth-century city.

Early humans gathered into communities for protection and mutual survival, then later, for purposes of politics, society, and economy. As they gathered, many civilizations began to "plan" their communities. The Egyptians, Greeks, and Romans took care to design and plan their cities for comfort, beauty and efficiency. The basic goal of city planning is **quality of life.**

During Romanesque and Gothic feudal society, cities and towns grew haphazardly, built about a central castle or monastery. There was little, if any, attention given to public utilities, plazas, parks, drainage systems and sewers, or paved roads. The towns did generate a rather attractive array of spontaneous spaces, but they were often unhealthy, dangerous, and inefficient.

44.1.

G

Some historical examples of excellent efforts in city planning include the Zahringen towns in Switzerland; Paris *(fig. 44.2)*; Bath, England; and the London of Sir Christopher Wren.

Today, cities like Brasilia; Chandigarh, India; Radburn, New Jersey; Vallingby and Farsta in Sweden; and new "oil communities" in the U.S.A. (Utah, Colorado, Wyoming) are examples of **totally planned** communities.

44.2.
Architect's rendering for Versailles; from *Urban Space* by J. S. French.

PRODUCTIVE THINKING

What are all of the things you would want to handle, improve, and provide if you were an architect beginning a new city?

How would you make a city that had unity, order, and harmony in design, yet interesting variations? (For example, if *all* of the buildings were round and domed, they would have much unity and harmony, but you might want relief from all of the roundness. What would be an obvious, perhaps too easy solution? What would be a **unique** way to give relief from all the domed roundness *(fig. 44.3)*?

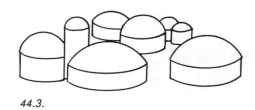

44.3.

Concerns of City Planning

Beauty of spaces
Water supplies and hygiene
Safety
Recreation, entertainment, play areas
Transportation (pedestrian, vehicle, rapid transit)
Green belts
Education
Churches
Hospitals
Museums
Shopping, banking
Hotels and public spaces
Garbage removal and disposal
Burial system
Energy efficiency and flexibility

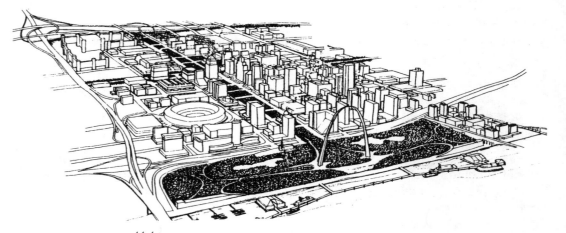

44.4.
Architect's rendering from *Urban Space* by J. S. French.

Cognitive:

1. Draw a city whose buildings are too much alike, or have too much unity.

2. Draw some things into the city which give it variety and interest without destroying the unity. In *figure 44.5* the lines of the row houses (too much alike) are repeated in the larger addition—size and angle providing **variety.**

44.5.

Divergent:

1. Make a plan for a small city (one each school, public building, police station, fire station, park, hospital, shopping center, church, etc.). Locate the buildings according to logical relationships of function.

2. Select one building from your plan and draw a picture of it.

3. Analyze community planning problems in your city. Are traffic patterns the best? How could they be improved if money were no object? If money *were* important? Use the lists from the productive thinking exercise to look for possible improvement areas. (In the city in which I reside, north-south traffic is designed to flow better than east-west traffic.)

4. Study *figure 44.6* to identify the concerns that were dealt with in this civic plaza.

44.6.
St. Louis Proposed Central Civic Plaza; Downtown St. Louis, Inc.; from *Urban Space* by J. S. French.

44.7

7/45

CONCEPT

Contrast can be used by architects to attract attention or to lead our attention progressively from one shape or form to another.

LESSON

"There is no perception without contrast." —Franklin Y. Gates

One of the most useful tools for a design is the knowledge that the human eye loves contrast *(fig. 45.1.).* Contrast is interesting; it has impact; it draws one's attention; and the eye cannot resist it.

As a gift requires a recipient, similarly, contrast must have something to contrast *with.* There cannot be one without the other.

If you had a design with a series of large rectangles, how could you create an entry that would be a center of attention? What would contrast with large rectangles? (Small circular or angular shapes, perhaps of differing texture or color.)

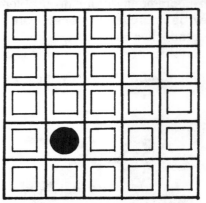

45.1.

C

Do you remember the problem which Frank Lloyd Wright encountered when designing the Morris Shop in San Francisco? The other businesses screamed and shouted for visual attention. Wright *got* the attention by **contrast.** He used a quiet, simple, rectangular wall and put one circular entry to its left. A contrasting line of protruding bricks leads the eye to that contrasting entry *(fig. 45.2)*. The simple facade is such a contrast to the visually active street that it arrests one's attention.

45.2.
Morris Shop (now Helga Howie Boutique), San Francisco; Frank Lloyd Wright, 1948-1949.

One of the architects who influenced Frank Lloyd Wright in design was Louis Sullivan. In 1914 Sullivan designed a bank in Grinnel, Iowa. How did he use contrast to make the entry a center of attention *(fig. 45.3)*? (By circularity contrasting with rectangles and by detail upon simplicity. The detail is the decoration on and above the entry.)

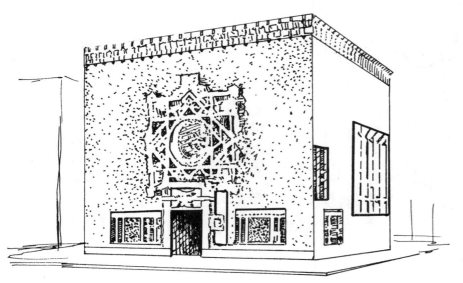

45.3.
Merchants National Bank, Grinnel, Iowa; Louis Sullivan, 1914.

What are some design elements that can be used for contrast?

Imagery: An image lacking contrast (too much like the other shapes and values) is nearly invisible. Can you see anything concealed in *figure 45.4?* This example involves contrast in the perceptual problem of **closure** (enclosure). *Figure 45.5* represents an aid to the solution.

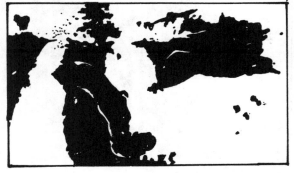

45.4.

45.5.

Figure 45.6 is a group of doors and entrances. Select one, and design a front (facade) with which the doorway can contrast in some way.

45.6.

COGNITIVE: A circle will contrast with a _____.

A yellow shape will contrast with a _____ shape.

A smooth surface will contrast with a _____ surface.

A light wall will contrast with a _____ entry.

Divergent and Convergent: Design a face for one of the entries in *figure 45.6*.

Find **contrast** in other areas of life, i.e., politics, clothing tastes, etc.

7/46

Order is the single most important general design concept in architecture.

"Order is basic. There can be no freedom without it." —Craig Ellwood

The opposite of order is **chaos** or **anarchy. Order** is the way various things relate to each other. As we learned in Lesson 1/2, one way to achieve order is by lining things up or grouping them *(fig. 46.1)*.

46.1.

B

There are other ways to perceive order, besides lining things up or grouping them. One of these ways is by symmetrical **balance** *(figs. 46.2 and 46.3)*. When the eye perceives that things are distributed evenly about a line or a point, it senses the order.

Another way order may be achieved is by **dominance** (hierarchy). In this case, dominance is a spinoff of contrast. By varying the size, shape, color, value, or placement of something, we give it attention-getting power.

Although one part of the composition controls or dominates the others, it also gives emphasis to the order about it. The Germans used the word **gestalt** to describe order or organizational essence, and architects and artists often use this term to describe the essence of order.

Disorder may be used positively in architectural design to relieve too much order, to give a "playful" feeling to the structure, or to express that kind of haphazard space we so enjoy in nature.

Another ordering principle spins off of **rhythm** or **repetition.** (See Lesson 1/7.) Repetition creates both pattern and rhythm. We can organize various elements by

repeating them as a pattern , lining them up (ranking) □ □ □ □ □ , or giving

them shape □ □ . This repetition principle moves away from purely linear rhythms.

A **continuum** can serve to maintain order. A line, planar slab, or volume may draw other elements around it *(fig. 46.4)*, as in grouping or patterning, using proximity as an ordering principle.

Transformaton is an imaginative way for architects to maintain both variety and order. Very subtle changes and manipulations may be made to strengthen existing orders. Transformation is a form of **elaboration** upon existing patterns and older ideas *(fig. 46.5)*. It may be romantic, ecclectic, or innovative.

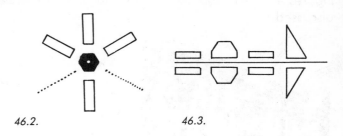

46.2.   46.3.

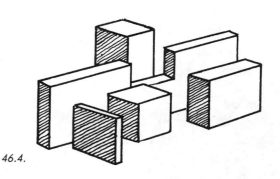

46.4.

46.5.

Figures 46.6 through 46.11 are some buildings **ordered** by principles we have discussed.

46.6.
Lining things up (ranking).

46.7
Symmetry. Tempietto S. Pietro, Rome; Donate Bramante, 1502.

46.8
Dominance. Taj Mahal, Agra, India; 1632-1654.

46.9.
Repetition (with dominance by size)

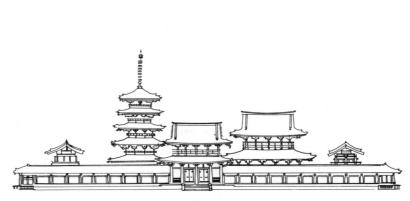

46.10.
Continuum. Horyu-ji Temple Compound, Nara, Japan; originally A.D. 607.

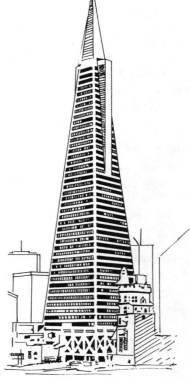

46.11.
Transformation. Transamerica Building, San Francisco; William Pereira Associates, 1972.

List all of the things in your room which are in order and tell which principle of order they use. (Is it linear, symmetrical, dominance, repetition, continuum, or transformation?)

Can you find **disorder?**

Similes: (Complete in your most imaginative way.)

When people are **disorderly,** they look like _____.

When a building is in order, you can easily tell because it looks as if _____.

Cognitive: Look through magazines and in nature to find examples of **ordered** objects. Determine which ordering principles are used.

Divergent: Create a design (using blocks, cardboard, drawing materials, construction paper cutouts) which you know to employ a particular principle of order.

Find examples in the neighborhood of social order, chaos, or anarchy.

7/47

Proportion may be enhanced geometrically by using regulating lines.

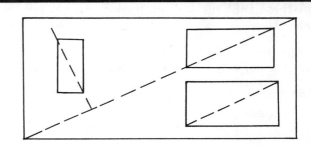

Renaissance architects used **parallel diagonals** to achieve a sense of order and proportion in their buildings *(fig. 47.1)*. Their discovery is still used by architects today.

The concept is simple enough to understand, but may be challenging to perceive in actual buildings.

Rectangular proportion has always been analyzed by the fact that a diagonal of a rectangle can be used to keep other sizes of rectangles in **proportion** to it. Each part (height, width, etc.) remains similar to all other parts, as well as to the whole.

Renaissance architects then discovered that if such diagonals were either parallel or perpendicular to each other, the proportional relationship would be similar. Such diagonals are called **regulating lines.** When such diagonals line up, the rectangles relate proportionally and the visual result is pleasant or harmonious *(fig. 47.2)*.

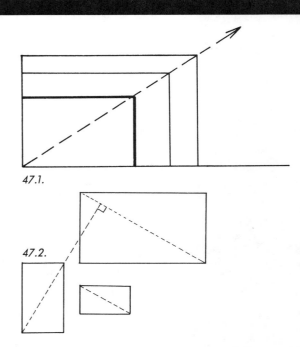

47.1.

47.2.

E

Figure 47.3 is an example of Sangallo's use of the principle for Palazzo Farnese in Rome. (The diagonals of all windows and bays are perpendicular to the overall regulating diagonal.)

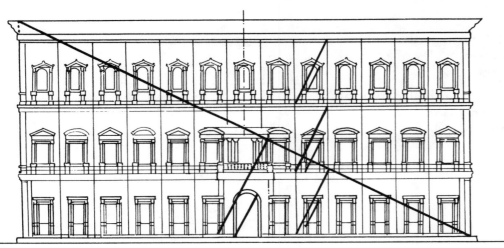

47.3.
Palazzo Farnese, Rome; Antonio da Sangallo, the younger, c. 1515.

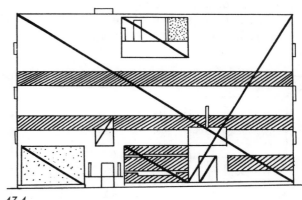

47.4.
Villa at Garches, Vaucresson, France; Le Corbusier, 1926.

In *figure 47.4,* the principle was used by a twentieth-century architect, Le Corbusier.

PRODUCTIVE THINKING

What is a diagonal? Why does a diagonal of a rectangle keep other lines on the diagonal in proportion?

What are some ways we can measure proportions of things by comparison with other things? For example, the human body is generally found in certain proportions. One of these is the eyes; they are halfway between the top of the head and the bottom of the chin, as in *figure 47.5.*

Another is that in many adults, there is a space between the eyes equal to the width of one eye *(fig. 47.6).*

An example of measuring proportion in architecture: How many stories tall is a tower or section of a building? (In *figure 47.7,* the building is four stories tall.)

Analogy: Proportion is to measuring as _____ is to _____.

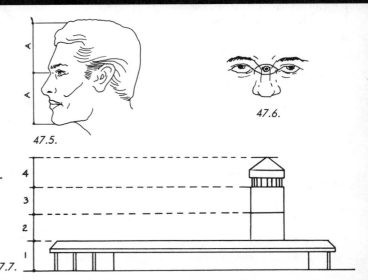

47.5.

47.6.

47.7.

Cognitive: Draw two rectangles of different size so that their diagonals are parallel *(fig. 47.8)*, or perpendicular, or both *(fig. 47.9)*. Begin with one, draw its diagonal, then make another to relate to it.

Divergent: Using rectangles cut from construction paper, create a design controlled by regulating lines, as in *figure 47.10*.

Study photos from art history books or of twentieth-century buildings, to see if any buildings indicate use of regulating lines. You may want to trace modules which have parallel or perpendicular diagonals (i.e., doors, sections, windows).

Consider and discover regulating lines in other aspects of life, such as boundary lines and gerrymandering, lines of demarcation, national lines, lines of "class" in some countries (caste systems to keep proportion of "haves and have-nots").

47.8.

47.9.

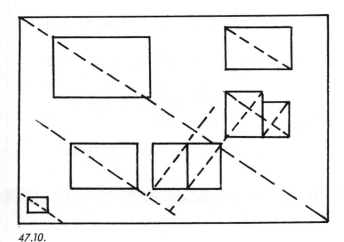

47.10.

7/48

To create more aesthetic designs, architects sometimes adjust the relationships between positive and negative spaces. When we move through those spaces we experience drama in architecture.

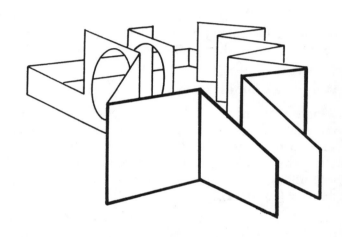

LESSON

Architects make decisions concerning **positive** and **negative spaces** (Lesson 5/33). They **adjust** those spaces to work more pleasantly.

In home building, planners quickly learned that standard 8-foot ceilings were inexpensive to build because everything could be cut to that length, or portions of it, and because a room with 8-foot ceilings was easier to heat and cool than one with 10-foot ceilings. The result was a home with all ceilings eight feet high, without variation. The negative spaces were visually boring. Architects again began to think about **space aesthetics** and **spatial drama.**

F

A good example of spatial drama lies within the traditional Gothic cathedral *(fig. 48.1)*. **Time** plays a role in this space relationship. As one approaches the cathedral entries, the large outdoor space with sky, clouds, and trees is experienced. Then, passing through the portals (doorways) into the narthex, the space has a low ceiling and is quite darkly lighted. One feels almost cramped and small. Next, looking through the portals into the nave one **senses** a new spaciousness, but it is not yet fully visible. Like experiencing chords and melody in music, one remembers the outdoor feeling of space, the cramped small narthex, and entering the nave—perhaps 10 stories high, a soaring vertical space—one's attention goes upward, almost to the infinite spaciousness of the outdoor experience, yet more contained, then back horizontally to the dramatic center of attention in the choir and apse where the altar is located.

In the story "Why the Chimes Rang," the author takes advantage of just such spatial drama as the setting for two little boys in Europe long ago. The cathedral and outdoor space is shown, then "little brother" is shown at the altar inside the grand cathedral.

Why the Chimes Rang

"There was once, in a far-away country, a wonderful church. It stood on a high hill in the center of a great city. It had a grand entrance leading to the main room, which was so long that one could scarcely see to the other end where the choir stood by the large altar. The great organ was in the farthest corner. The tower of the church rose so far into the sky that it was only in very fair weather that anyone claimed to be able to see the top *(fig. 48.2)*.

"At the top of the tower was a chime of Christmas bells. But the fact was that no one had heard them for years and years. One old man said that his mother had spoken of hearing them when she was a little girl. It was the custom on Christmas Eve for all the people to bring to the church their offerings to the Christ child; and when the greatest offering was laid on the altar, the Christmas chimes would ring.

"A number of miles from the city, lived a boy named Pedro, and his little brother. They knew very little about the Christmas chimes, but they had heard of the service in the church on Christmas Eve, and had a secret plan to go and see the beautiful celebration.

"The day before Christmas was bitterly cold, the walk was hard in the frosty air, but by nightfall, Pedro and his little brother could see the lights of the big city just ahead of them. They were about to enter one of the gates, when they saw a poor woman who had fallen in the snow just outside the city, too sick and tired to go on to shelter. Pedro knelt down beside her and tried to rouse her. He turned her face toward him so he could rub some snow on it. Then he said:

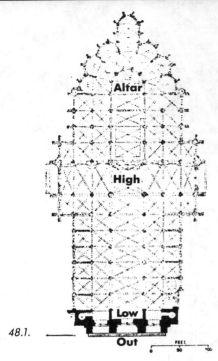

48.1.

48.2.

'' 'It's no good, Little Brother. You will have to go on alone. See this poor woman. She will freeze to death if nobody cares for her. Everyone has gone to the church now, but when you come back you can bring someone to help her. I will rub her to keep her from freezing, and perhaps get her to eat the bun that is left in my pocket.

'' 'Both of us need not miss the service. You go and see and hear everything twice— once for you and once for me. I am sure the Christ child must know how I should love to come with you and worship Him; and oh! if you get a chance, Little Brother, to slip up to the altar without getting in anyone's way, take this little silver piece of mine, and lay it down for my offering when no one is looking.' In this way he hurried his reluctant little brother off to the city and winked hard to keep back the tears.

''At the close of the service came the procession with the offerings to be laid on the altar. Rich men and great men marched proudly up to lay down their gifts to the Christ child. Last of all walked the king of the country, hoping with all the rest to win for himself the chime of the Christmas bells. The people murmured as they saw the king take his royal crown from his head and lay it on the altar. 'Surely,' they said, 'we shall hear the bells now.' But still only the cold wind was heard in the tower. Some doubted if they ever rang at all.

''The procession was over, and the choir began the closing hymn. Suddenly the organist stopped playing, and the minister raised his hand for silence. As all the people strained to listen, there came softly the sound of the chimes from the top of the tower—so much sweeter than anything that had been heard before, that the people in the church sat for a moment not moving. Then they all stood up together and stared at the altar, to see what great gift had awakened the long-silent bells.

''But all that the nearest of them saw was the childish figure of Little Brother, who had crept softly down the aisle when no one was looking, and had laid Pedro's little piece of silver on the altar.'' *(Fig. 48.3.)*

48.3.

Suffice it to say, the spaces are dramatically interesting. Compare this to the undramatic unity of having all ceilings eight feet high. This is an example of how talented architects create more aesthetic designs by adjusting the relationships of the positive and negative spaces.

Study *figure 48.4.* How has the architect adjusted positive and negative space using sculptural forms?

48.4.

As we learned in Lesson 5/33, positive and negative spaces may be designed to interchange. Look at the image in *figure 48.5*. What do you see? (Is Abraham Lincoln positive or negative?)

48.5.

Figure 48.6 is a drawing of what it looks like to walk around the Transamerica Building in San Francisco. How are the shadows like the building structure? Which is positive, the shadow or the pavement? What shapes are the pavement (light) shapes? Has the architect used positive and negative space in an interesting way? What has he used for positive forms? (**I**-beams, columns, triangulation, etc.) What are all of the shapes you can see here?

Simile: If an architect never thinks about negative spaces, his positive spaces will
_____. (Be like doughnuts without holes, holes without doughnuts?)

48.6.

Cognitive: Using tracing paper, trace buildings by outlining only the negative spaces. Do any visual changes or moods occur? What if the negative spaces are made positive, and the positive spaces made negative?

Divergent: Create a toothpick (or straw or balsa wood, etc.) sculpture, and stretch **planes** of tissue paper over parts of it by gluing them to the toothpick shapes *(fig. 48.7)*. Analyze the arrangement of positive and negative shapes. Which are more interesting? (They should be equally interesting.) You are in the act of adjusting the positive and negative spaces.

Consider tunnels as negative space, and explore how **functional** negative spaces are. We live in them, move through them, and react to them.

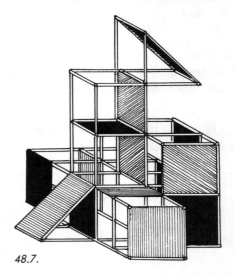

48.7.

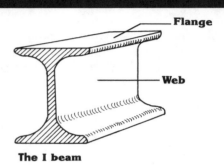

Flange

Web

The I beam

Many important parts of common structures and building processes can be named.

There are thousands of specific terms that apply to a building and its structural materials. It will be helpful to learn the names of a few.

The first thing an architect does is make working drawings or **plans,** also called **blueprints, blue lines,** or **brown lines.** He draws a **site plan, floor plans,** and **elevations** *(fig. 49.1)* (indicating foundations and footings; structural framing; mechanical, plumbing, and lighting details; and special plans for rooms, cabinets, built-ins). Architects today can actually draw plans on computers designed to produce such graphics.

The architect has specifications typed up (a detailed written description of materials, equipment, sizes, quality, and performance dates for a builder). These are called **specs.**

The builder then uses the plans and specs to make a **bid** *(fig. 49.2)*—written offer to build the building for a certain fee. Usually the low bidder is awarded the job. He is then called the **contractor.**

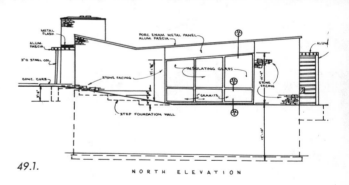

49.1.

NORTH ELEVATION

$

49.2.

The builder takes the working drawings to make measurements at the property *(fig. 49.3).*

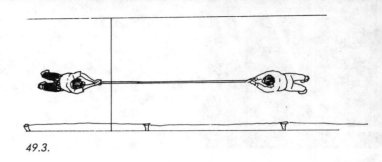

49.3.

After the measurements are **staked out** and surveyed, a **subcontractor** is called to make **excavations.** His machinery quickly and easily digs the excavation holes exactly where the builder has put the stakes and string lines *(fig. 49.4).*

49.4.

After the excavation, the holes or trenches for the footings are dug and filled with gravel and concrete *(fig. 49.5).*

49.5.

After the footings have **cured** (dried), the **foundation** forms are constructed and the concrete poured. The first floor is ready to be **framed in** *(fig. 49.6).*

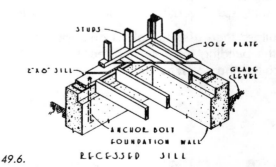

49.6.

Figure 49.7 is a **wall section,** indicating parts of a brick veneer house (outside brick, inside wood and plaster).

Figure 49.8 is a house being framed up on the foundations. No brick or siding has been put on, so all studs, braces, joists, and rafters are visible. What style roof will it be? (Gabled.)

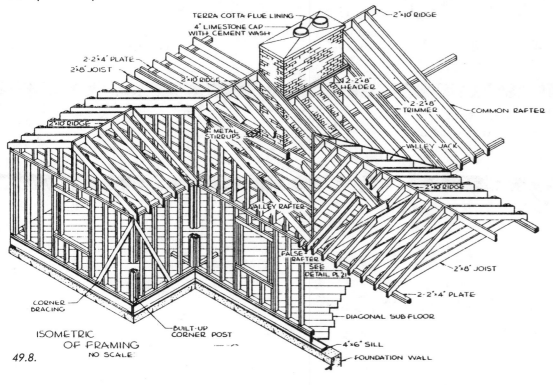

ISOMETRIC OF FRAMING
NO SCALE

49.8.

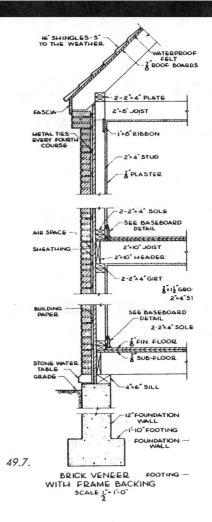

49.7.

BRICK VENEER WITH FRAME BACKING
SCALE 1/2" = 1'-0"

A stairway consists of **rail, balusters, treads,** and **risers** *(fig. 49.9).*

If there is a lot of overhang on the **eaves,** as in *figure 49.10,* a **soffit board** is nailed under the exposed rafters. A **fascia board** covers the ends of the exposed rafters.

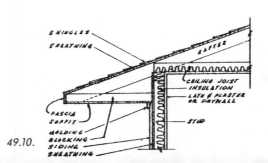

49.10.

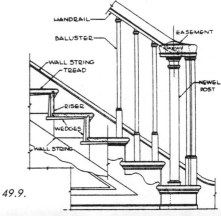

49.9.

Figures 49.11 through 49.15 show a few of the most common brick patterns used on walls.

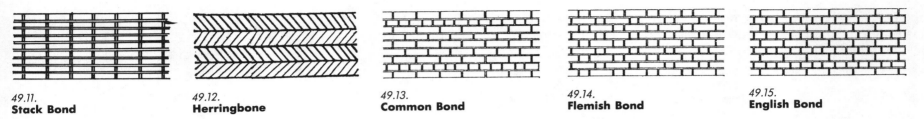

49.11.
Stack Bond

49.12.
Herringbone

49.13.
Common Bond

49.14.
Flemish Bond

49.15.
English Bond

Cognitive: Visit a home or building under construction. Identify ten structural parts. Do not choose *general* ones such as flooring, door, or window. Find joists, trusses, runners, strings, headers, studs, jambs, soffits, and so on.

Divergent: Design a bricking pattern you have not seen before. Try it with wooden blocks.

CONCEPT

The building site and government building codes influence the architect's plans for the buildings and landscape.

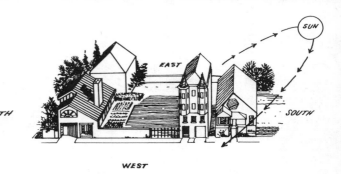

LESSON

Most homes in the later twentieth century have been built in neat, tidy rows with front doors all facing the same direction as those of neighboring houses. Many of these homes have back yards or play and garden areas.

Increasingly, builders and architects are realizing that buildings should be oriented so as to be comfortable in hot and cool temperatures, and to be protected against winds. Sometimes winds in **summer** can be used to cool the house *(fig. 50.1)*, yet the house can be oriented to ''brace itself'' against **winter** winds.

50.1
Summer Cross Ventilation.

When sun is to be used for heating (or cooling), the **site plan** is very important. *Figures 50.2 and 50.3* indicate how the sun's rays approach the house at different angles at different times of the year. Windows facing south collect the most **solar energy** during the winter months because the sun is low in the sky. During the hot summer months, a small overhanging eave on the roof will keep the high summer sun from coming directly in through the windows.

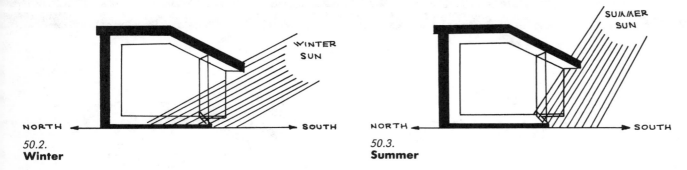

50.2.
Winter

50.3.
Summer

The architect must consider the **topology** of the site. *Figures 50.4 and 50.5* diagram a small house set on a flat and a sloping site.

The architect orients the structure to enjoy the best possible **view** from the windows, porches, and patio.

50.4
Flat site, partially bermed.

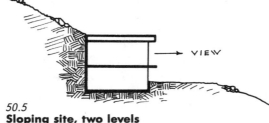

50.5
Sloping site, two levels

Landscaping must be carefully planned to control sun, wind, and view, and to be productive. Trees and bushes must be planned so that their roots do not get into sewer, water, or drainage pipes *(fig. 50.6).*

50.6
Bermed-up sides with trees giving shade in summer but allowing sun to penetrate in winter. Evergreens provide a wind screen.

The architect should plan pleasant relationships with **neighboring architecture and environment.**

The architect draws **plot plans** to show how to **orient** a home on the site. *Figure 50.7* is an example of a plot plan of levels, and *figure 50.8* is a plot plan of landscaping.

Soil samples are dug to find out the bearing capacity, drainage, water table, landscaping needs, etc. (Rocks are grand for footings, but *not* so grand for growing trees and plants. Sandy soil is not good for heavy foundations but often has good water drainage capacity.)

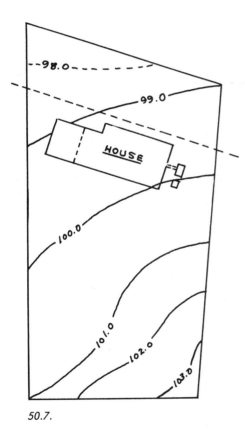

50.7.

50.8.

What are all of the things an architect should consider when planning how his/her building will fit the site? Consider your own home or apartment building. How could it have been better oriented to its site? In what ways is it oriented "just right"?

Analogy: A site is to a building as a _____ is to a _____.

Plan a two-room house to be built in your neighborhood and oriented to receive the sun's rays in the winter but not in the summer, and to be braced against winds in the area.

Draw simple plans for a house on a hillside *(fig. 50.9)*. Cut into the hill if you wish. Where will you put the entry? Where will you have windows and porches or terraces with a view?

How would this house be different from a house built in the desert?

Look at ways other cultures or people have solved site problems. Inspect (from library books, movies, etc.) Navajo hogans, pueblo cities, ancient cliff dwellings, the ancient ruins in Peru, Dutch canal cities, and Venice as sites. Consider jungles, beach cities, and so on. How did architects and builders relate these buildings and cities to those sites?

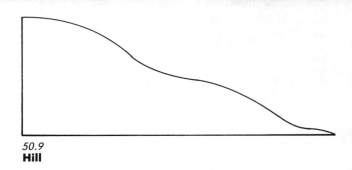

50.9
Hill

''The infinite life of the arts is sparked by faith; an unchangeable essence, regardless of wars, interruptions, or neglect, the arts outlive governments, dogmas, and the cultures which produce them. Because they are the essence of reality they cannot be totally destroyed. They are the true historians—all that is left when the dust and ruins are cleared away.''

—Nathan B. Winters

Time lines in this appendix are keyed to the lessons by an identifying letter, A-M. Find the appropriate time line in this appendix and read the explanation of how it relates to the particular lesson you are studying.

A

Pyramid of Cheops, Egypt, 2600 B.C.
Mortuary Temple of Queen Hatshepsut, Egypt, 1500 B.C.
Stonehenge, Great Britain, 1650 B.C.
Treasury of Atreus, Mediterranean, 1300 B.C.
Etruscan Temple, Pre-Roman, 500-400 B.C.
Tomb at Caere, Pre-Roman, 500-400 B.C.
Pont Du Gard, Rome, 118 B.C.
The Pantheon, Rome, 118 B.C.
Ise Shrine, Japan, A.D. 300
Kondo, Japan, A.D. 600
El Castillo, Chichen Itza, Yucatan, A.D. 800
Temple of the Sun, Mexico, 1500
Castello Nuovo, Naples, 1260
Milan Cathedral, 1380
Santa Maria della Consolazione, Italy, 1545
Farnese Palace, Italy, 1535
Brighton Pavilion, Great Britain, 1815
House of Parliament, Great Britain, 1835
Crystal Palace, Great Britain, 1850
Eiffel Tower, France, 1880
TWA Terminal, New York, 1962
Seagram Building, New York, 1956

Used in Lessons

1/1 Alike and different   The buildings are arranged in pairs to be either alike or different.
2/10 Pattern   Every building on this line uses a pattern or repetition of motif.
3/13 Contrast and emphasis   Every building has points of emphasis, from entry to roof.

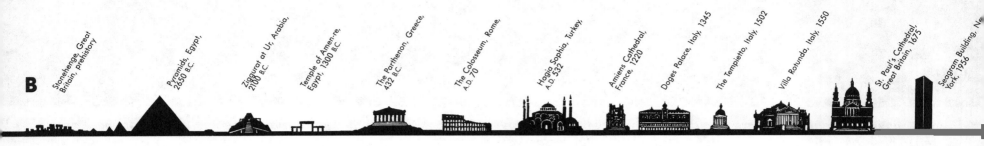

Identification

Stonehenge   massive stones arranged in circular order corresponding to the sun, moon, solar equinox, etc.
Pyramids   a triangle motif on a square base facing the compass points, the ratio of height to perimeter base is "pi"—3.1416.
Ziggurat at Ur   stepped pyramid on symmetrically ordered ramps and stairs.
Temple of Amen-re   a hypostyle hall with stone posts and beams arranged on the order of a grid system.
The Parthenon   a temple with mathematical order—even number of columns, double on the sides, using the golden proportion of $1:1\frac{6}{10}$.
The Colosseum   an amphitheatre using an order of arcades and oval design.
Hagia Sophia   ordered with large central dome surrounded radially by smaller supporting domes with minarets at each corner of the square site.
Amiens Cathedral   ordered into Gothic mathematical divisions—three doors and three stories, symmetrically placed towers, etc.
Doges Palace   ordered arcade on each floor.
The Tempietto   a restatement of ancient classical orders on circular motif to herald the Renaissance.
Villa Rotunda   use of classical orders but with creative license.
St. Paul's Cathedral   use of classical orders—symmetrical, calculated proportions.
Seagram Building   simplicity and ordered proportion using a grid system.

Used in Lessons

1/2 Order   Each building on this time line is in order by its repeated shapes and sizes.
1/7 Rhythm   Every building on the line uses rhythm in its design in some way.
3/16 Function and form   Every *great* building uses forms which fulfill a function—either to collect solar energy, allow movement, gather light, shade, etc.
4/21 Rhythm, pattern   Each building has a studied use of repeated forms in windows, roof, structure, etc.
4/22A Styles and periods   Nearly every building will eventually fit into a style or period. A few will remain totally unique.
4/23 Orders of architecture   Each building on the time line exhibits a classical order in terms of columns, pediments, or proportions.
5/37 Structure is geometric   Each building capitalizes on basic geometric forms and shapes.
7/46 Order   Every building has order by mathematics, historic precedent, proportion, or similarity.

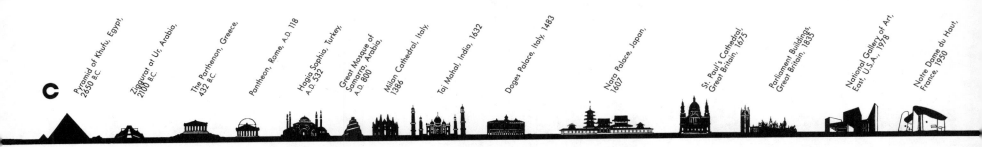

Pyramid of Khufu, Egypt, 2550 B.C. · Ziggurat at Ur, Arabia, 2100 B.C. · The Parthenon, Greece, 432 B.C. · Pantheon, Rome, A.D. 118 · Hagia Sophia, Turkey, A.D. 532 · Great Mosque of Samarra, Arabia, A.D. 800 · Milan Cathedral, Italy, 1386 · Taj Mahal, India, 1632 · Doges Palace, Italy, 1483 · Nara Palace, Japan, 1607 · St. Paul's Cathedral, Great Britain, 1675 · Parliament Buildings, Great Britain, 1835 · National Gallery of Art, East, U.S.A., 1978 · Notre Dame du Haut, France, 1950

Used in Lessons

1/3 Edges Any person, object, or building may be recognized by its silhouette or edges.

2/9 Balance Buildings, blocks, and things may be arranged with formal and informal balance.

3/17 Geometric form and nature These buildings are very geometric in form. (Fuller's Geodesic Dome is the last building on the time line for this lesson.)

3/19 All views These buildings are beautiful and interesting from every view.

3/20 Weight These buildings have dominant forms or optical weight.

5/34 Mass The silhouettes of buildings on the time line show that mass is usually roof shapes or wall spaces.

5/35 Formal and informal Each of these buildings is designed either symmetrically or asymmetrically.

6/38 Pattern Each building has used pattern in its wall surfaces.

7/41 Line Each building picks up a form and is horizontal or vertical due to extended points and planes.

7/45 Contrast for focal point Each building has a definite contrasting point of visual interest.

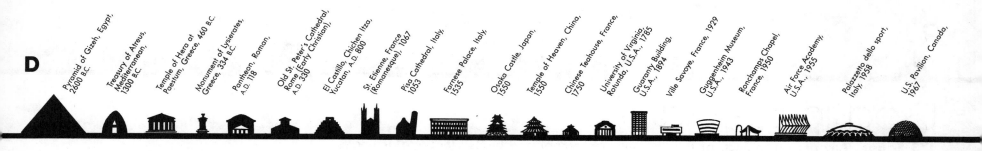

D

Pyramid of Gizeh, Egypt, 2600 B.C.

Treasury of Atreus, Mediterranean, 1300 B.C.

Temple of Hera at Paestum, Greece, 460 B.C.

Monument of Lysicrates, Greece, 334 B.C.

Pantheon, Roman, A.D. 118

Old St. Peter's Cathedral, Rome (Early Christian), A.D. 330

El Castillo, Chichen Itza, Yucatan, A.D. 800

St. Etienne, France (Romanesque), 1067

Pisa Cathedral, Italy, 1053

Farnese Palace, Italy, 1535

Osaka Castle, Japan, 1550

Temple of Heaven, China, 1550

Chinese Teahouse, France, 1750

University of Virginia, Rotunda, U.S.A., 1785

Guaranty Building, U.S.A., 1894

Ville Savoye, France, 1929

Guggenheim Museum, U.S.A., 1943

Ronchamps Chapel, France, 1950

Air Force Academy, U.S.A., 1955

Palazzetto dello sport, Italy, 1958

U.S. Pavilion, Canada, 1967

Used in Lessons

1/4 Basic Shapes/Forms   Each building uses distinct basic geometric shapes and forms.

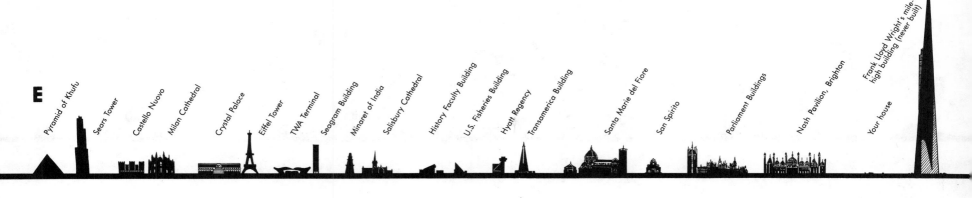

E
Pyramid of Khufu
Sears Tower
Castello Nuovo
Milan Cathedral
Crystal Palace
Eiffel Tower
TWA Terminal
Seagram Building
Minaret of India
Salisbury Cathedral
History Faculty Building
U.S. Fisheries Building
Hyatt Regency
Transamerica Building
Santa Marie del Fiore
San Spirito
Parliament Buildings
Nash Pavilion, Brighton
Your house
Frank Lloyd Wright's mile-high building (never built)

Used in Lessons

1/5 Size   Buildings may be compared in size. Compare Frank Lloyd's mile-high building to all the others.

2/11 Measuring   Every building may be compared for measurement to other buildings or objects.

3/18 Scale   These buildings have widely varying scale relationships to humans and to each other.

5/28 Proportion   Every building here is to a planned proportional relationship.

7/47 Proportion   Every building on this line has well studied proportional relationships of parts to the whole.

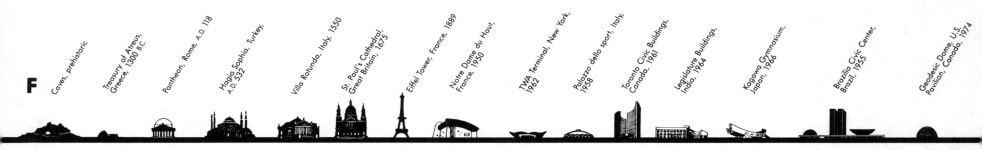

F — Caves, prehistoric — Treasury of Atreus, Greece, 1300 B.C. — Pantheon, Rome, A.D. 118 — Hagia Sophia, Turkey, A.D. 532 — Villa Rotunda, Italy, 1550 — St. Paul's Cathedral, Great Britain, 1675 — Eiffel Tower, France, 1889 — Notre Dame du Haut, France, 1950 — TWA Terminal, New York, 1962 — Palazzo dello sport, Italy, 1958 — Toronto Civic Buildings, Canada, 1961 — Legislature Buildings, India, 1964 — Kagawa Gymnasium, Japan, 1966 — Brazilia Civic Center, Brazil, 1955 — Geodesic Dome, U.S., Pavilion, Canada, 1974

Used in Lessons

1/6 Built environment All buildings, town, bridges, monuments, parks, highways and so on are part of our built environment.
4/25 Convex and concave Every building in this line has a convex or a concave curvature in its form.
5/33 Positive and negative space Each of these structures uses a ''play'' of positive and negative space.
6/40 Shadow Each building changes character according to the time of day and how it uses light and shadow at that hour.
7/43 Color Every building in our environment has colors which must relate to other colors around them.
7/48 Relationships, positive and negative space Each building on this line has well analyzed relationships of positive and negative space.

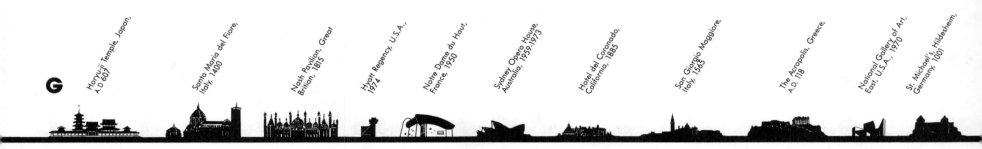

G Horyuji Temple, Japan, A.D 607 · Santa Maria del Fiore, Italy, 1400 · Nash Pavilion, Great Britian, 1815 · Hyatt Regency, U.S.A., 1974 · Notre Dame du Haut, France, 1950 · Sydney Opera House, Australia, 1959-1973 · Hotel del Coronado, California, 1885 · San Giorgio Maggiore, Italy, 1565 · The Acropolis, Greece, A.D. 118 · National Gallery of Art, East, U.S.A., 1970 · St. Michael's, Hildesheim, Germany, 1001

Used in Lessons

2/8 Units and clusters All of these structures combine multiple forms, yet achieve unity.

2/12 Unity, relationship Every building combines forms in a unified relationship.

3/14 Site and environment Every building occupies a site. Not all occupy it well. These do. (The Parthenon is the last building on the time line for this lesson.)

4/26 Variety Each of these buildings uses a touch of variety to make at least an entry more interesting.

5/29 Golden mean Every building is to a planned proportional relationship. (The last three buildings on the time line for this lesson are the Pantheon, the Tempietto, and Palazzetto dello sport.)

7/42 Groups and clusters Each complex clusters towers, roofs, separate structures, and other forms into a pleasing whole.

7/44 City planning Buildings become one another's environment, and therefore, cities should be planned.

7/50 Site The sites of these buildings have been considered very important in the design concepts.

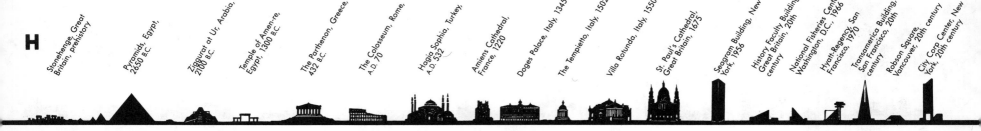

H — Stonehenge, Great Britain, prehistory · Pyramids, Egypt, 2650 B.C. · Ziggurat at Ur, Arabia, 2100 B.C. · Temple of Amen-re, Egypt, 1300 B.C. · The Parthenon, Greece, 432 B.C. · The Colosseum, Rome, A.D. 70 · Hagia Sophia, Turkey, A.D. 532 · Amiens Cathedral, France, 1220 · Doges Palace, Italy, 1345 · The Tempietto, Italy, 1502 · Villa Rotunda, Italy, 1550 · St. Paul's Cathedral, Great Britain, 1675 · Seagram Building, New York, 1956 · History Faculty Building, Great Britain, 20th century · National Fisheries Center, Washington, D.C., 1966 · Hyatt-Regency, San Francisco, 1970 · Transamerica Building, San Francisco, 20th century · Robson Square, Vancouver, 20th century · City Corp Center, New York, 20th century

Used in Lesson

3/15 Planes   Every building on this line is a composite of planes.

Log cabin · Dutch Colonial · New England Colonial · French Colonial · Georgian · Hogan · Federal · Greek revival · Spanish Colonial · Gothic revival · Italianate · Stick · Eastlake Victorian · Shingle style · Craftsman, Greene and Greene · Bungalow · International · Solar

Used in Lessons

4/24 Homes in your community These are a few chronologically ordered homes found in our world.

5/36 Roof recognition Each home has a unique roof style.

7/49 Parts of structures Every building has numerous named parts which become the vocabulary of building.

Identification

Stonehenge   symbolic of the zodiac, the seasons, etc.
Pyramid of Khufu   symbolic of the Egyptian caste society, sun worship.
Ziggurat at Ur   symbolic of stepping to heaven.
Temple of Amen-re   decorated with symbolic writings.
The Parthenon   temple symbolic of order in beauty, culture, society.
Great Stupa   domed canopy of heaven.
The Pantheon   symbolic of sun worship, zodiac, heaven.
Hagia Sophia   asymbolic of sun worship, zodiac, heaven.
El Castillo   symbolic of stepping to heaven.
Muktesvar Temple   symbolic sculpture on surface.
Chinese pagoda   symbolic of nature, tree, and cardinal principles of Buddhism.
St. Michael's   symbolic of Christian austerity and strength.
Amiens Cathedral   decorated with symbols of Christianity, rose window = all-seeing eye.
Santa Maria Novella   Christian symbols, Renaissance interest in classical orders of God.
The Tempietto   symbolic of Renaissance (rediscovered classic orders) and proportion.
Crystal Palace   impressionistic use of light in architectural structure.
Temple Square   surface carved with religious symbols.
Notre Dame du Haut   reputed to be symbolic of European nun's hat, cubist use of light.
Sydney Opera House   symbolic of nautical motif (shells, sails, sea).
TWA Terminal   symbolic of bird in flight.

Used in Lesson

4/27 Symbolism   Each building form symbolizes nature, life, or societal values.

K

Used in Lesson

5/30 Special needs, special design All are examples of special functional requirements in design.

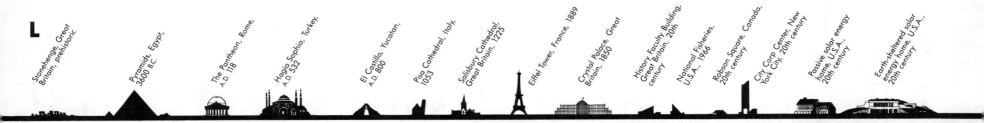

Used in Lessons

5/31 Solar, light and shadow   Each building was designed to emphasize and use light.
6/39 Simplicity   Great buildings utilize a sensitive balance between complexity and simplicity.

Identification

Stonehenge   effort to harness sunlight by worship.
Pyramids   Preservation from sun's rays by temperature control.
The Pantheon   hole in dome (oculus) controls sun's rays into drum of dome; nature worship.
Hagia Sophia   shade vs. light for temperature control and worship (canopy of heaven)
El Castillo   sun worship; height to get close to the sun.
Pisa Cathedral   Romanesque control of shade in hot Italian summers.
Salisbury Cathedral   Gothic play of light and shade on surface and through large window tracery.
Eiffel Tower   Impressionist play of light through arch form.
Crystal Palace   Impressionist play of light using greenhouse effect.
History Faculty Building   uses light to enhance study and research.
National Fisheries   reflects natural life-giving sunlight into the interior.
Robson Square   berms itself with controlled natural light and temperature control.
City Corp Center   allows solar energy to enhance the form of the structure itself.
Passive solar energy home   heated by the sun; heat is moved by rising warm air.
Earth-sheltered solar energy home   heated by the sun and wood-burning stove, insulated by earth.

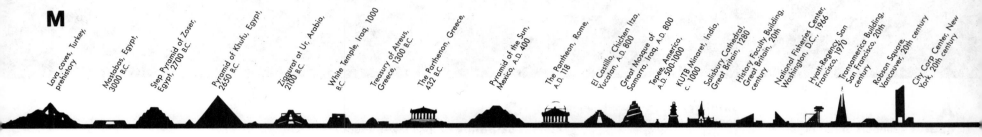

M

Lava caves, Turkey, prehistory

Mastabas, Egypt, 3000 B.C.

Step Pyramid of Zoser, Egypt, 2700 B.C.

Pyramid of Khufu, Egypt, 2650 B.C.

Ziggurat at Ur, Arabia, 2100 B.C.

White Temple, Iraq, 1000 B.C.

Treasury of Atreus, Greece, 1300 B.C.

The Parthenon, Greece, 432 B.C.

Pyramid of the Sun, Mexico, A.D. 400

The Pantheon, Rome, A.D. 118

El Castillo, Chichen Itza, Yucatan, A.D. 800

Great Mosque of Samarra, Iraq, A.D. 800

Tepee, America, A.D. 500-1000

KUTB Minaret, India, c. 1000

Salisbury Cathedral, Great Britain, 1280

History Faculty Building, Great Britain, 20th century

National Fisheries Center, Washington, D.C., 1966

Hyatt-Regency, San Francisco, 1970

Transamerica Building, San Francisco, 20th century

Robson Square, Vancouver, 20th century

City Corp Center, New York, 20th century

Used in Lesson

5/32 Triangles Every building on this time line exhibits stability through use of the triangle.

A

abacus   support at top of column for architrave to rest on.

active solar energy system   uses additional energy, such as electricity, to sustain the heating/cooling system.

altar   table or pedestal to hold objects of worship, or used for kneeling, praying, and in ordinances.

apse   the space at the end of the cathedral nave, usually round in form, used to house the choir and altar.

arcade   a repetition of arches lined up for a porch or roof over a portico, side aisle, or structural system.

arch   a span, usually circular or eliptical in nature, often using a keystone.

architrave   the straight span supported by columns in a typical classic facade.

articulated   sculpted, carved, or penetrated, as in an articulated wall surface.

atrium   an enclosed courtyard or garden area.

B

balustrade   a classical banister, or railing, used along a cornice, balcony or staircase.

baptistry   a structure housing a baptismal font or pool deep enough to fill with water so the clergy can immerse a religious initiate or convert under the water.

barge board   a piece of board similar to the fascia, which is hung to roof gable as it projects beyond the end wall, often covering the rafters. The barge boards may be decorative and usually meet at the ridge point of the gable.

balustrade   a banister above cornices.

basilica   a structural system employing a high central space (nave) flanked by side aisles.

battlement   the top of a wall with indentations along it, originally used to hide behind while shooting arrows, and later guns, to defend the castle or structure.

bay   a protruding window, allowing a more peripheral view.

beam   a span supporting a roof or floor, usually from wall to wall or post to post.

bracket   a support designed to strengthen a beam.

bungalow   a house style from the early 1900s (1910-1940) employing brick, hipped roof, and prairie-style motifs.

buttress   a wall support usually built by thickening the wall or attaching another wall or arm to the first wall.

C

campanile   a bell tower, usually part of a cathedral or church complex.

cantilevered   a span in a state requiring no support at one end because it is supported by weight or rigidity at the other end.

capital   the decorative top of a column.

caryatids   columns in classical design employing female sculptural form.

classical   the analyzed, calculated forms used in Ancient Greece and Rome.

clerestory   the upper portion of a wall, filled with windows to allow light to fill the upper portion of the room.

cognitive   understanding, ''catching on,'' comprehending.

collar beam   a wood beam with triangulated truss system, employing brackets.

colonnade   a porch lined with columns supporting its roof.

colonettes   small or delicate columns.

column   a post; a support to beams or roof systems.

concept   a cognitive principle or fact; the basic building block of knowledge.

continuum   a line of objects or ideas in some repeated sequence.

cornice the roof overhang, generally the edge.

court the flat, porchlike yard enclosed by walls for protection, privacy and comfort.

cresting ornamental member(s) used to form a decorative finish at the top of a structure (as along the ridge of a roof) as an elaborate coping (wall cap), or the top of a pinnacle.

cubist abstraction of form for the sake of composition, using simplified geometric shapes.

cupola a cup-shaped roof over the main part of a structure; a dome.

curvilinear using arches, curves, undulations.

D

divergent creating many alternatives or solutions as opposed to choosing only one "correct" solution.

dome the form resulting from spinning an arch like a compass. Usually it is a hemisphere or a variation of one.

dormer usually a gabled or hipped setting for an attic window; may also refer to a sleeping room or dormitory.

drum the cylinder supporting a dome.

E

eaves the beam ends creating a cornice; the lower portion of a sloping roof, near the wall but projecting beyond as an overhang to drip the water away from the walls.

echinus usually in Doric columns, it is a structural and visual "cushion" between the necking at the top of a column and the abacus block at the top of the column capital.

elevation the straight-on view of a building showing no sides, no perspective. It is useful to dimension and measure sides of a building accurately.

entablature the top of a classical structure above the columns, including architrave, frieze, and any horizontal mass, carried by the columns extending up to and including the first projecting cornice or drip moulding.

entasis the bowed or curved sides of a column to give the appearance of straight sides.

F

facade the front of a building.

fascia the edge of a cornice on a house.

finial a knob or elaborate ornament on top of a spire or pinnacle. The finials crowning the pinnacles of Gothic churches are often elaborate and beautiful.

flying buttress the support leaning against the barrel vault of a Gothic nave to control the thrust of the vault arches.

formal balance usually symmetrical or radial arrangements, balanced uniformly on each side of the center axis.

frieze the decorative span above the columns and architrave in classical architectural form.

G

gable the triangular-shaped roof.

gambrel roof the barn-shaped roof popularized in Holland.

garland a wreathlike decoration with vines carved in wood or stone, formed in plaster, or painted.

geodesic dome a dome invented by Buckminster Fuller, made entirely of light metal bars, connectors, and glass or thin coverings.

gestalt a holistic or overall view of something—more general in nature than detail oriented.

girder a structural member acting as a beam, usually in steel.

golden most excellent, as in golden mean, golden rectangle, etc.

greenhouse effect the maximum use of light penetrating a structure, usually attained with thin metal structural webbs holding glass panels.

H

hemispherical a form which is half a sphere.

hipped a roof system based on gables, but with slanted or beveled ends.

hypostyle a stone post and beam system developed in Ancient Egypt.

I

informal balance asymmetrical arrangement in which balance is achieved with unlike forms, or forms of varied weight or force.

K

key stone   the parallelogram-shaped stone which drops into place at the top of an arch, allowing the rest of the stones or voussoirs to rest against it.

L

lantern   the little structure at the top of a dome acting as a counter thrust to the dome's arches.

lintel   small beam over an opening, carrying the weight of the wall above it.

logo   an identifying symbol, in place of words.

M

mansard roof   a roof style developed in France, which has a flat or nearly flat top but steeply beveled sides.

masonry   structural system using walls or slabs of rock or brick or similar materials, usually held together with a mortar mixture.

mass   the main forms in a structure, .ie., a "chimney mass" or "roof mass."

metope   spacing between triglyphs in classical friezes, just above the architrave and colonnade.

minaret   a tall tower at the corners of the walls surrounding mosques, used for the purpose of calling Moslems to prayer.

module   a regularly spaced grid or sized construction section in a building.

moulding   a decorative piece of lumber from one to four inches wide and about an inch thick, which is used around floor edges, door jambs, and ceilings to conceal openings or cracks from construction.

N

narthex   an entry area in a cathedral using a double door effect; useful in controlling temperatures, providing a gathering spot and setting before entering the nave.

nave   the high, main space in a cathedral, facing an altar, where the congregation can gather.

necking   the ring at the top of classical columns, which begins the capital resting above it.

negative space   the background, air, or portion of a design which is created by objects, walls, lines, or positive forms.

notan   an Oriental science of arranging positive and negative space in such a way that it is difficult or impossible to tell which shape is positive and which is negative.

O

oculus   a round opening at the top of a dome, often a tension or compression ring, which allows light to come into the domed space or for a lantern/cupola to be built on top of the dome.

onion dome   a dome using the ogee principle of double curves.

origami   Oriental art of paper folding and cutting to make unusual abstract forms, usually flowers or birds or geometric forms.

P

palazzo   Italian for palace.

passive solar energy system   a heating/cooling system powered by sunlight and using no other energy sources, such as electric or gas-powered engines or fans.

pavilion   a gathering area for audiences or crowds, usually roofed but with no side walls, or roofed in a tentlike way.

pedestal   a substructure upon which a column, statue, or monument is raised. The term is extended to mean such substructures interposed at long intervals of a balustrade, sometimes but not always supporting a vase or statue.

pediment   the triangular gable of roof sloped over the front and rear of a classical building (Ancient Greek or Roman).

perceptual thinking   a synonym for visual thinking. It is non-verbal thought, using mental pictures based on past observation or percepts.

pilaster   an engaged pier with a more or less flat face, projecting out from a wall, usually having a capital, base, and so on. It corresponds to attached columns.

pinnacle   a subordinate vertical structure, usually masonry but sometimes wood, tapering to a point, usually crowning a buttress, ridge, or roof crossing.

pitched   applying to roof systems which are sloped to shed water or snow melt.

podium a continuous pedestal with a die, cap, and base used to elevate columns or monuments above the ground level. Roman temples were often built upon a podium, unlike Greek temples built on a stylobate or stepped platform.

portico a porch or vestibule, roofed but partly open on at lease one side, as in a cloister. Usually it is an ambulatory covered by a roof which is supported by columns on one side, as in classic temples.

positive space the space we can touch, feel, and see as actual object, as opposed to negative space which is background, or simply air in many cases.

post a vertical support for beams or other structural members.

proportion the relation of one part to another and to the whole, usually with respect to size and position or spacing. Often just height, width, and length relationships. It deals with dominance, balance, subordination and harmony.

Q

quoin the stones which go up the corners of the walls in a building.

R

rafter a roof beam; one of those which are set sloping from the ridge down to the wall plate.

rectilinear rectangle shapes.

relief sculpted or carved portions of stone, wood, or plaster which are raised or embossed so as to show decoration or images.

ribbed usually applying to domes or vaults, this term is used to identify the structural arches in those structures.

rose window the round, stained glass windows at the ends of the nave or crossing in Gothic churches.

rotunda a circular or cylindrical hall, especially one covered by a dome or cupola, like the Pantheon.

S

sculptural a modeled, articulated form; in architecture, the structure has indentations, projections, texture, shadow, and definition.

shed roof a roof sloped in one direction.

serpentine lines or forms, such as walls, which curve and undulate rhythmically.

shaft the main part of a column.

specs written specifications and definitions to clarify the drawn plans of a building. Specs are most useful for clarifying questions for contractors making bids, and for legal problems which later need resolution.

spindle small pieces of turned wood or stone turned into small posts in a banister.

stucco a cementlike plaster used as a covering for walls, put on wet and allowed to dry very hard.

stylobate a continuous stepped porch or base upon which a row of columns is set (the base of the colonnade).

T

tensile the quality of stretch or tension.

tower a tall structure, usually narrow, as a bell tower or a watch tower.

transom the bar of stone or wood which spans a door or window, usually supporting a small, often rounded window called a transom light or window.

transept a large division of a building which lies across or perpendicular to the building's main axis. In Christian churches, the intersection of main axis and transept is called the *crossing.*

triglyph a three-grooved stone in the frieze of a Doric ordered classical building symbolizing a wood beam end.

truss a framework of timbers or metal bars, etc., interlocking to become a light but rigid beam to roof or span large areas or openings. A truss is usually based upon a series of triangles.

turret a small tower, especially one attached to a larger tower.

V

vaulted the state in which a series of arches touch or are ''roofed'' so as to create a tunnel.

veranda an open gallery or portico covered by a roof, supported by pillars or columns, attached to a building's exterior walls.

villa a country residence or house—set in orchards, gardens and groves.

voussoir one of the many stones used to form an arch or rib on a vault in a wedge shape.

volute a spiral scroll or "ram's horn" shape to a capital of an Ionic classical column.

W

wing a part of a building projecting from but subordinate to the central or main part.

Z

ziggurat an ancient step pyramid having long, stepped staircases up its front and sides, usually found in ancient Ur, or Babylonia, now Iraq.